THE ULTIMATE SCRIPT BOOK

FOR NETWORK MARKETERS

NEVER WONDER WHAT TO SAY AGAIN
OR HOW TO SAY IT

BY: ROB SPERRY AND BRIAN FRYER

THE ULTIMATE SCRIPT BOOK

FOR NETWORK MARKETERS

**NEVER WONDER WHAT TO SAY AGAIN
OR HOW TO SAY IT**

BY: ROB SPERRY AND BRIAN FRYER

TGON Publishing

TGON Publishing

© 2021 TGON Publishing. All Rights Reserved

Reproduction or translation of any part of this book beyond that permitted by Section 107 or 108 of the 1976 United States Copyright Act without written permission of the copyright owner is unlawful. Criminal copyright infringement is investigated by the FBI and may constitute a felony with a maximum penalty of up to five years in prison and/or a $250,000 fine. Request for permission or further information should be addressed to TGON Publishing.

Warning—Disclaimer

The purpose of this book is to educate and inspire. This book is not intended to give advice or make promises or guarantees that anyone following the ideas, tips, suggestions, techniques or strategies will have the same results as the people listed throughout the stories contained herein. The author, publisher and distributor(s) shall have neither liability nor responsibility to anyone with respect to any loss or damage caused, or alleged to be caused, directly or indirectly by the information contained in this book.

CONTENTS

INTRODUCTION 9

1 STRATEGIES 19

2 FIRST INTERACTIONS AND SIMPLE INVITES 27

3 FOLLOW-UP 45

4 OBJECTIONS 61

5 CLOSING PROSPECTS 69

6 SOCIAL MEDIA SCRIPTS 73

CONCLUSION 105

"You can't make a good movie out of a bad script."

— George Clooney

INTRODUCTION

As a self-proclaimed movie expert, I have seen how a bad script can ruin a good storyline. George Clooney nailed it when he said this about scripts. My wife and I went to a movie we were both excited to see for date night. As we watched the movie, I could tell that the plot was there, but unfortunately, the script was terrible! After the movie, I turned to my wife and said, "I want someone else to take that same plot and rewrite the script!" So much potential was wasted with a lousy script.

I see this happen in network marketing, too. The basis for the business, the opportunity, and the product are all amazing! We have one of the most successful, resilient industries in the world. So why don't more people join? Frequently, people don't know what to say. They get so nervous and afraid of what to say and how they will be perceived that they don't even want to try.

It's like they are on a movie set in front of the camera, without a script or direction and the director yells "ACTION." Some people may give it a try and fumble through it. Eventually, they may learn what to say and how to deliver it if they keep doing this. Some people fumble and get so embarrassed that they never try again. Some of the most fearful people completely freeze and never say anything. You have likely seen this happen in network marketing.

As a successful network marketing coach with over a decade of experience coaching, hosting masterminds and speaking worldwide, I help people find success and then help duplicate that success with their teams. One of the biggest roadblocks I see for so many people is getting stuck with the HOW. "How do I engage with someone I have never connected with?" "How do I invite someone to a call with my sponsor?" "How am I supposed to take a casual conversation and start talking about my business?" "How can I feel confident in any situation I am in?" This book is the answer to all of those questions and more. You will no longer worry about what to say in every situation in conversations related to your business.

When I retired from being part of any network marketing company, I started my coaching business. I now get to coach, speak, consult, and host mastermind events for all different levels of people in network marketing. I also help dozens of companies on the corporate level of network marketing with creating systems and consulting. The combination of my personal experience in the industry and coaching thousands of others has shown that success in network marketing comes from doing the basics better.

I can teach anyone how to do all of the skills in network marketing. They are basic. But what truly creates success is doing the basics better. You must learn how to master the basics. One of my good friends and a fellow network marketing coach, Brian "Coach" Fryer, and I discussed the fundamental principles of network marketing. We agreed that talking to people, whether in person or online, was the

INTRODUCTION

most BASIC skill people need to learn to succeed. Both Coach and I are passionate about helping people learn to master these skills, and we soon realized as we continued to talk that we needed to write a book together, and now this book is now in your hands.

Coach Fryer and I love being able to help people in network marketing learn how to do the basics better. He has helped his clients learn how to talk with people by using essential, indirect scripts that give them the knowledge to learn what to say and how to have conversations. Coach Fryer said, "Scripts help you get over the fear of not knowing what to say and lets you focus on helping others." When Coach said this to me, the idea for this book came to mind. We would write a book together that focused on helping people in network marketing learn how to do the most BASIC thing better.

We believe in the power of words. There is a right and wrong way to talk to people. We are passionate about teaching people the RIGHT way to talk to people. It is hard to make a sale or get someone interested in a business opportunity if you don't know how to speak to them! The most fundamental principle is learning to talk to people to get to know, like, and trust you. This isn't just about customers, but everyone.

This book has been a collaboration from the beginning. From professional baseball player to an online business mentor, Coach Fryer teaches network marketers how to turn their organic content into sales while making an impact! He happens to be a MASTER when writing and implementing scripts into network marketing, especially those who want to build on social media.

Brian is a husband, father to four kids, and a faith-driven coach. Everything he teaches is what he did to become the #4 income earner in his last company, building 100% on social media. He is also an

THE ULTIMATE SCRIPT BOOK

author and wrote one of the best books on building an online business. You can check it out at www.CoachFryer.com/book.

Through his membership, masterminds, and personal mentorship, Coach Fryer has helped tens of thousands of network marketers worldwide grow and scale their business online. He`s known for taking the most challenging obstacles his clients face and making them SIMPLE. With his degree in psychology, he knows how to mentally get the most out of his clients so they can make the most significant impact possible.

Coach Fryer is the founder of the Social Impacter movement. He was featured as one of the TOP 16 social media influencers at a recent online summit. He has also been highlighted at the Association of Network Marketing Professionals event on the social media panel of experts. Recently Coach Fryer was the social media keynote speaker at TWO of the fastest up and coming direct sales companies in the United States.

The value that he offers and his experience is unmatched in this industry. Brian and I have collectively added the foundational scripts for ultimate success! We will cover what to say on social media, how to interact with people in person, how to handle objections, and the list goes on and ON. Consider this book your script bible. Something you will open up daily and reference time and time again with each new season of your business. You can see why I had to write this book with him! Neither Coach Fryer nor I am part of any network marketing company, nor will we ever be again. We are committed to YOU and the entire profession. We love watching you succeed! If you have AH HA! moments and you find scripts that are helping you have success in this book, tag us on social media @robsperry and @coach_fryer. We want to celebrate with you!

Does anyone else have a LOVE/HATE relationship with SCRIPTS?

In network marketing, scripts are so valuable. They help take the guesswork out of what to say for the newest person who is afraid or worried that they will say the wrong thing, OR even worse, not say anything at all. Think back to the example of making a movie. It's hard to create a successful film with no script or a terrible script.

There are proven scripts and formulas that have withstood the test of time to help every person in network marketing enroll more, stay more actively engaged, and connect with team members and leads. Scripts also help the newest person succeed and win faster than ever before while helping REDUCE the risk of being rejected. Being rejected in any capacity is the ultimate killer of one's belief.

When I, Rob, started network marketing, I loved scripts because I had no clue what to say or do. I wanted a script! I wanted to be told what to say to show people I knew what I was talking about. I also didn't love the discomfort of not knowing what to say next.

I also hated scripts because people would repeat the script word for word. It made them sound too robotic and not authentic. Too many network marketers confuse principles and techniques. They think they need to repeat word for word what the script says. Scripts can occasionally make people sound like they are doing a terrible acting exercise. Applying a good script means you extract the principle being taught and use it with your style and personality. People are buying YOU, so the script needs to be adjusted to how you would say it and your personality. Don't miss out on an opportunity because you took a script, read it word for word, and forgot to make it yours.

MY mentor was incredible. He had a powerful personality, and he approached people and said something like this, "I am going to make a ton of money, so give me your credit card so that you don't miss out." This simple direct approach created both boldness and fear of loss. This script worked for him. The approach was contrary to my style and personality. If I had tried to use that script word for word, it would have come off as arrogant and inconsiderate. I learned the principle behind his successful approach and applied it to my style and personality. No one taught me a script for me to approach others. It took me figuring out what the bold version of me would say. I had to try and tweak it until I found what worked best for me.

I became the #1 recruiter out of a million distributors and built my business in forty-plus countries before retiring from building and committing to coaching. Coach Fryer and I are committed to YOU and the entire profession's success as coaches and mentors in this industry. As you read each script and section, your focus should be applying the principles using your own words and tone.

Borrow from your past success. Almost all of you have had success at something in your life. Whether in music, sports, school, or a job, find something you have excelled in. For most, people, too hard on themselves, thinking that success means you have to have been the very best. That's not the case. Pause for just a moment, and think about something you worked hard at and became much better at? Progress is a success. Progress comes from deliberate action and teaches you how to excel at anything. Now use this example to bring you instant credibility. Both Coach Fryer and myself played sports at top levels, and we would both constantly use that past success to sell to our future successes. For example, we would take the same work ethic and determination we both had on the court and field and apply it to our network marketing businesses.

Now that's an elementary example on purpose. You can expand it and choose the words that fit your style. You can go more in-depth on what you did before and what you will do to have future success. Use strategy one as well to combine both for a very powerful invite.

Remember, scripts are meant as a guide. Maybe you will use the script word for word, but frequently the script is meant as a guide and framework. We have provided a basic framework for you later in this book to give you an idea of what makes a good script work. It will always sound better if you add your personality and own words to the script. Neither of us would start a message by saying, "HEY GIRL!", but maybe you do! That is what is going to take these scripts to the next level. Be willing to be yourself and add YOU into the scripts we have given you.

The principles we are teaching you through these scripts work! Remember, most communication is non-verbal, so the magic to these scripts is more than just the words. Don't worry; we will teach you more than just the right words to use in scripts. This is the most comprehensive teaching on scripts you have ever come across and it will help both you and your teams tremendously. We will dive into all of the different scripts and, more importantly, the principles behind them so that you can apply them to your style and personality, but first...

A quick housekeeping item

In my first four years in network marketing, I joked that "compliance" was the sales prevention program. I was partially joking but primarily serious because I felt like they wouldn't allow us to say anything at all.

I later learned that compliance is crucial to your business. Compliance helps you build a business that is not only successful but in line with best business practices. Compliance keeps your company out of

THE ULTIMATE SCRIPT BOOK

trouble with the regulators, but even more importantly, it can help you create a culture that doesn't attempt to take shortcuts with hype and misleading claims.

Every company in network marketing has a compliance team that you can contact and ask questions to. As you build your business, make sure you utilize your compliance team to ask questions and learn the best practices for staying compliant in your business. Please read through the policy and procedures of your company to learn what you can and can't say.

How we have set up this book

One of the main things that hold people back from having a successful network marketing business is what to say and when. These scripts help take the guesswork out of the conversations. We hope you will use this and share it with your teams as they are learning more about having different conversations with people.

This book is set up to guide all conversations in network marketing. People may read it cover to cover, but this book is meant as a resource that you can go to the table of contents when you need some help, flip to the script you need, and use it as that conversation comes up with prospects. This will be a tool you use to train and coach your team to learn how to do the basics better.

We will be sharing the different scripts, adding some teaching principles, sharing experiences we had had using scripts, and showing you best practices for using scripts throughout this book. You will see that we have a specific section for social media. We found these scripts work best on social media, but please remember that *scripts are guidelines*. USE IT if you find a social media script that works for you in person! We have spent years perfecting and coming up with these scripts so that you can have the most success in network marketing. In section one, we have shared strategies to help you grow in your network marketing business. We both use fundamental principles and strategies we shared in section one to help our clients become even more successful in their businesses.

Now that we have clarified the expectations of this book, how to use it, and best practices, let's begin!

"The capacity to learn is a gift; the ability to learn is a skill; the willingness to learn is a choice."

– Brian Herbert

SECTION 1

STRATEGIES

There are several strategies to consider implementing as you go through these scripts. Make sure that you are using the scripts and testing out how they work and constantly adjusting them to your personality to get the highest success rate for you and your team.

There is a framework used to create effective scripts for messaging and making connections with new people. The framework includes: Intro, compliment and question.

The example below is for a first connection with someone online:

Intro (Hey __Name__!)

Compliment (I loved your suggestions on detoxing, I am looking forward to implementing what you shared!)

Question (Do you have any other suggestions for a newbie?)

First, make an intro. Use the person's name and introduce yourself. Give them an authentic complement of something you know about them, and then ask them a question. Here is another example using the framework, "Hey Mary! I love your suggestions on detoxing; I am looking forward to implementing what you shared in your post the other day. Do you have any other suggestions for a newbie?" We will share several different scripts that can be used in many instances through this book, but the framework will always be used.

The Direct Invite vs. The Indirect Approach

The number one question we are asked when it comes to scripts and networking online is, "Should I be direct with people and make an offer right away, or is it better to be a bit more indirect and form a relationship first? Which is better?"

We did a study with seriously committed network marketers and asked them, "How long did you know your sponsor in network marketing before you signed up?" The results were inconclusive.

- One hundred seventeen knew their sponsor for over a year.
- Forty-four said they were directly messaged right away.
- Forty-three said they knew their sponsor for 1 to 3 months.
- Ten said they knew their sponsor for 4 to 8 months.
- Seven said they knew their sponsor their entire lives.

The range of the results makes it clear that there is no one way! We can't tell you exactly how to do this or which way is better. You have to try a mix and see what works best for YOU. This doesn't mean to be a spammy pammy, but you need to try different methods and track the results.

The main principle to understand is to be the bold version of YOU. In a perfect world, we would approach others how they would want to be approached. The issue with that is how can we know how they want to be approached when we barely know them? We can't, so you should approach others how you would want to be approached. Think about what you have to offer and how you want someone to talk to you about the product or opportunity. This creates what I call "The authentic share." The goal in all networking is to be authentically you and help people solve a problem. If you try to "FORCE SHARE" by doing it in a way that doesn't feel authentic, you will have little success or quit because it won't feel right.

Some people hate when others approach them in the first direct message. If I were to tell these people to pitch directly from the first message, they would HATE IT! It wouldn't feel authentic, and it would be a task they dreaded because they hate when people do that to them. They would either send messages that felt odd or not send anything at all because they disliked it so much. This ultimately doesn't do any good for anyone. YOU should feel CONFIDENT in the approach you feel is best. You may feel awkward stepping out of your comfort zone, but knowing you are saying something that YOU would say will help to make this process less awkward.

The opposite can also be true for others. If you hate when someone doesn't get straight to the point, you will not feel authentic if you wait to approach others about your business or products. The "authentic share" is all about doing business the way that feels best for you. The best way to find your own "authentic share" is to ask yourself, "How would I want to be approached about this?" As you read this, star or highlight items, you feel aligned with and make notes to tweak it to find your authentic share.

Let's talk about the notorious spammy pammy. If you approach someone on the first message, you are spamming them. NOTICE, I didn't say the first conversation. There is a HUGE difference. Don't be spamming people in the first message. Your success rate will dwindle, and your reputation online will be shot. But, don't wait too long. If you wait longer than three messages to bring up your offer, you are stalling in your business. We both came up with something called "The rule of contact" This rule says DO NOT offer on the first message with people. People will not engage with you in the first message with an offer. They will believe that all you want is to sell them something. The sweet spot is in the second message. The second message lets you establish a connection with people and get to the point of one reason you reached out.

As mentioned, messages and conversations are different. A message is a DM or "direct message" in someone's inbox on social media platforms. Conversations happen outside of the inbox. These happen in person, on a post thread, in text messages, etc. Conversations are unscripted ways of interacting with people. When we talk about conversations, I don't care if you approach someone during the first conversation, second conversation, or third conversation as long as it isn't the first message or after the third conversation.

BE the BOLD VERSION OF YOU! Don't jump right in and not be curious about other people. But don't sit around having fourteen conversations and NEVER talk about your offer. Find your sweet spot. Our challenge for you is to start using the rule of contact and see how it works out for you. If you have been in this industry for a bit, you can probably look at your list and see a couple of contacts that you are stalling—time to jump in and make that offer.

THE SPLIT TESTING METHOD

This method has been used in the online world for years and will be a game-changer for your network marketing business. Split testing uses traffic segmentation to randomly distribute visitors between two different URLs of the same page to determine which one performs better. In other words, the same website URL you click sends half of the traffic to one side and the other half to a similar website to see which one converts better. Each site will have something slightly different, and that is what you are testing. You are trying to gauge if one particular content, photo, or offer is getting a higher close rate than the other. The minor changes matter, but we won`t know if we don`t test them.

For example, if you go to www.bookbundle.robsperry.com to get my books, you may get one of two different websites. It is random. My website will track which one converts better. Sometimes it is just a simple font change or even just one image that makes a huge difference. Split testing helps you make minor adjustments that can add up to huge returns.

Split testing works the same way with scripts. Every single person operates differently. To know what is working in your scripts, you will want to do a split test to see what script is outperforming the other. The key is to make slight adjustments, not change the entire script. Scripts work so differently for each person, so just split test! Split test the direct and indirect style messaging. Another thing you can split test is track inviting 30 people more directly and 30 people more indirectly. Split test everything you can!

Let`s say the indirect is the best approach for your style and personality. Now start to approach 30 people with one script and 30 with another with minor variations. Let`s say that with script A you have 22 out of 30 interested and seven that sign up. Now let`s say with script B, you have 14 out of 30 interested and two sign up. You have a clear winner and actual data. One of the keys to split testing is to tracking your numbers. Data is how we adjust and create personal scripts that have a considerable return and that you feel confident in using. Think about it. This is how a traditional business would operate. This is how you need to operate your network marketing business as well. Our friend Bob Heilig often says, "If you don't know your numbers, you don't have a business; you have a hobby."

Never stop split testing! Even if you have found a better script, you can still try others. I work with some of the most successful people in network marketing, and they are all split testing all of their content and offers. This is one of the critical tools that successful people and businesses use.

One of my multi-million dollar earning clients takes script A, which performed better the first time, and studies and assesses to see WHY it did better. She then uses the information and creates a NEW script B to see if she can get the new script to outperform the other one. Now test scripts A and B, inviting 30 people using each script. This provides a new data set to work from. She has now created scripts that have over an eighty percent closing rate using split testing! Who wouldn't LOVE to get those types of results?! If you continue to do this every time, you will find the best wording that fits your unique style and personality and become the BOLD version of YOU. Just remember, don't fall into the trap of over analyzing the data. Set a specific number you plan to test and evaluate the results from each after the goal has been met.

This SPLIT TESTING METHOD alone will be the game changer for your business, but only if you apply it. Everyone says how DEEP their why is, but I always ask, "Do your actions match your why?" Your why may be profound, but if the actions don't match, your why is only a dream that makes you feel better. Use split testing, the authentic share, and the rule of contact to consistently take action and adjust.

The rest of this book will give you strategies and principles to accelerate your learning curve and your success! I highly encourage you to get your friends and team members learning these principles with you asap! That's how you achieve accurate duplication and leverage.

Social media has changed the game as far as connection and broadening your reach in the world. We have found that your network and who you can connect with have exponentially grown since social media. In the next section, we will talk specifically about scripts and principles on social media.

Testing, getting feedback, and adapting your scripts will be the fastest and best way to succeed. Even if you have been in this business for ten years, you will want split testing with your content and scripts. The market changes, as does social media, trends, and how we interact with people should always stay up to date.

Taprooting

Taprooting is something that often gets overlooked when expanding your network. Think about it...how often have you enrolled someone who may have enrolled a few others, but then the original person you enrolled quits or leaves? This happens more often than we think, but what about those people they brought in? They now feel stranded and maybe even abandoned. Taprooting will help you continue to build AND help those stranded people see that all is not lost if their sponsor quits.

What is taprooting? Taprooting is the art of working through people. You aren't working through people in the way some may think. Some think you sponsor someone to get to the next person only to abandon the person you sponsored. This is not the case at all. You support your team to continue building and reaching out to their network. Taprooting is getting into someone else's circle of influence to help strengthen the team. It is one of the best ways to create duplication.

We will share a couple of strategies that help you continue to build while using taprooting within your team.

1 - Have a system in place that will help you to be able to PERSONALLY connect with each new team member. This business is about relationships, and you want everyone to feel like they are creating and building a relationship with you. You can connect with a Facebook group, Voxer, Telegram channel, or even email. The key is to establish that initial connection as quickly as you can.

2 - Once you begin building your team, you need to recognize where the fire is! Who are the rockstars, and HOW can you support them even more? We suggest reaching downline and speaking with them to avoid potential conflicts between you and their sponsor. Taprooting will help them offer additional support and communication, which can be incredibly beneficial to you and your team.

3 - Taprooting is a tool that we use to continue supporting and building the people who want to build their business. Set up easy ways for you to support and help the newest person by doing things like having scripts ready, doing three-way calls, etc. Taprooting is a continuous tool that you will be using. Make sure you are using it!

You are sponsoring through getting into someone else's circle of influence. Some studies say that if you know five people, you know the entire world because we are connected. Learn to become better and better at getting into other people's circle of influence, and you will never run out of contacts.

SECTION 2

FIRST INTERACTIONS AND SIMPLE INVITES

Before you make an offer or invite anyone to check out a business opportunity, you must first interact with that person. This is called the first interaction. So many people get weird about this! Often people say that they don`t know how to talk to people and don`t know what to say. The most important thing to remember is to stop overcomplicating this! Remember, anyone can overcomplicate things; it takes a genius to keep it simple! When you first talk to someone, it isn`t about the business or your product. The first interaction is about saying hello and getting to know a little about the person. Don`t worry; there`s an entire section about how to do first interactions, invites, and follow-ups on social media later in this book and you can always refer back to the framework for ideas and simplicity. This section is about in-person interactions. Remember that all scripts can be adjusted and used however you see if they make the most sense for you.

Once you have completed the first interaction, you can start moving into an invite. This may happen naturally in the first conversation, or it may be a couple of conversations in. The key here is not to stall. It takes BOLDNESS to make an invite. Remember that it will always be a "no" if you don't ask. Below we have included scripts for first interactions with several people and groups. You can use these scripts when inviting and making the first offer to people. REMEMBER our rule of contact. Below we have included first and second interactions with people. The first interaction is always going to be to make a connection. The second interaction is where the offer will come in.

You will interact differently based on the different relationships you have with them. Your friends and family want to help you, but they may not want to sign up with you. That's ok! You can still utilize them for networking and even practicing what to say (hello split test). But a word of warning, don't ASSUME that they aren't interested. Give everyone a chance to say yes!

The best part about family and friends is that you already know each other, and you don't have to set a baseline with them. Make sure you stay interested in them while still inviting them to look into what you are doing. Start by asking them how things are going or what they have been doing. You can then use one of these scripts for the invite to introduce someone to the products as a customer.

Don't keep yourself small by just talking to family and friends. You have to branch out of that group and talk to other people. This includes strangers in person and online, people you know at work, and anyone else. We sometimes get in our way when we start to have thoughts and worry about what people will think of us. It is not what you say but the intent behind the words that matter. Before the first conversations or invites, remind yourself of WHY you want to start these conversations. That will always help to stay focused on what matters. We have shared with you loads of scripts to get the conversations started.

FIRST INTERACTIONS AND SIMPLE INVITES

Another group of people that you will want to include is people that you haven't spoken to in years. Let me tell you a story about Jared. We will use the name Jared because that's his real name (that was a joke, but it is true). Jared messaged me, wanting to catch up. I was pretty excited that this long-lost friend wanted to catch up with me.

We talked for a good 30 minutes about everything. At the end of the 30 minutes, he let me know that he had become a financial planner and wanted me to be a client.

So what was the problem? I was excited to catch up with Jared, but I felt used. I felt like he didn't really want to catch up with me and only cared about making money off me. It took all of that excitement that I felt when I heard from him and deflated it all because he was only "catching up" for his financial gain.

Many feel this way about approaching them about our network marketing business or products, and things can become awkward quickly. The bummer about the whole thing is that there is a correct way to reach out to people we haven't talked to in several years AND share our opportunity.

There may be people that you want to connect with that have WAY more credibility than you do. Maybe they have a successful business or have a substantial social influence that you don't have. So many people stop short of making offers to people they think are more credible and imposter syndrome kicks inStop making yourself the issue. When you are worried about what someone thinks of you, you are selfish! It's ok; it can even be great to work with better people than you.

Not even Jesus was liked by everyone; why do we think we should be? Next, stop selling yourself short. I once had a client that wanted to approach a successful entrepreneur. She kept telling herself that he would never give her the time of day and that she had nothing

29

to offer him. It turns out she was SO WRONG! When she got over selling herself short and approached this man, he told her he had been following her for a while and was excited to pick her brain about a couple of things—win/win for both. Get over yourself and start approaching people with more credibility than you.

The scripts for the first interaction with a stranger (In-person)

"Hey _____! I know this might sound completely crazy as we barely know each other, but I've enjoyed seeing your posts the last few weeks and was curious if you'd be open to learning how I'm making some extra money online? If not, no worries."

"Hi _____. I believe we have some mutual friends. Do you know ____(insert friend's name)? That is so great! How do you know them?"

"Who do you know at this event?" They will answer, and then your following response connects to them. "I went to high school with them!" OR whatever the connection is.

"I love this spot. What brings you here?" Use their answer to connect.

"Tell me a little bit about yourself. Do you love what you are doing right now?"

The first interaction with a close friend or family member (products)

"Hey ____, I know this is random... I'm doing a bit of research. Would you mind answering a couple of questions?"

FIRST INTERACTIONS AND SIMPLE INVITES

"Do you or someone you know struggle with any of these?" (insert pain points that your ideal client is struggling with. This can be a list of 5-10 things your products help with).

"Hey _____. I wondered if you would be willing to help me out with something. *(Wait for them to respond before proceeding)*

I've got a new product I'm starting to market, and I am looking for people I can trust that are willing to TRY it out and share their feedback for my portfolio.

(Briefly explain the product and the problem it helps solve, i.e., pain, stress etc., back pain, etc.)

Would you be willing to try it for 60 days-maybe, COMPARE it to whatever you are currently using and let me know what you think?

If you don't like it, I'll never ask you to buy it again. But if you love it (I think you will), It comes with a 60-day money-back guarantee, so if you don't like it for whatever reason, you have no risk to try it."

"My goal is to make (insert your real goal) within the next three years (insert time frame). I know everything worthwhile is always harder than we think. I will do whatever it takes, even if it takes me longer than three years (reinsert the timeframe you mentioned earlier)."

"I would love to have your support as I do this business differently this time around. Would you be willing to jump on a call on (date/time) to hear more about this company?

"Your support means the world to me. I appreciate you being here through it all. I know this will be a long-term commitment to myself, my business, and I would love your support. Would you be willing to jump on a call and give me your honest feedback?

The scripts first Interaction to businesses

"What's up _____? What are you doing (date/time)? I found a way for us to make some money! There is a quick video that explains the details. If I give you the link, will you watch it?"

"Hey _____. Listen, I've decided to take on a new entrepreneurial direction. I just found a great business with a different kind of company. This is an all-natural and all-organic company from Europe that is pre-launching in the US. I was lucky enough to be contacted by one of the top money earners of the company to take a look, and I'm in. I don't care if you do this. I only care that you look. Will you do me a favor and take a quick look for me?

Great, watch this quick video – will you watch this video for 5 minutes so I can link you into the big picture with the top guys – (promote upcoming influencer call/meeting)"

"Hi_____. I love seeing the great business doing_____. I have found a great company that would be a great addition to what you are already doing. It could be a great way to make more income by doing exactly what you are doing right now. If I send you a link, would you take a look?"

"Hi _____!. I love following you on (insert social platform). I would love to connect and talk specifically about what we both have been up to this past year with the business. When does it work best for you?"

The scripts first interaction with neighbors or co-workers

"Hey Mary! It looks like you had a great (4th of July, Christmas, Memorial Day, Labor Day, Birthday, etc.) What's new with you?"

FIRST INTERACTIONS AND SIMPLE INVITES

"Hey _____. You popped in my head today and I thought I would see if you could help me with something I'm working on right now. How is your week going?"

"I am getting ready to launch one of the biggest businesses in our lifetime, and you were one of the first people that came to mind because I know I can count on your support. This may or may not be for you, and I promise I wouldn't waste your time if it weren't something I thought you would be interested in or know someone that would be. If you aren't interested, I won't ask you again, but I think you might know someone else that this could be for. I have partnered with a successful mentor that is helping me get started. Your consideration and taking a look would mean the world to me. Are you available at (insert date/time) to show up and ask questions to help me with my training?"

Please note the difference between hype and passion. It is a fine line, but if one truly believes this is one of the biggest businesses in their lifetime, they need to find a way to share that excitement.

"Mr/ Mrs _____ what are you doing (date/time)? I'm working on a business project, and I am looking for a few sharp people to partner with. You've always been good at (insert compliment). Are you open to taking a peek at another stream outside of what you are doing now?

The scripts first interaction when you have been in multiple network marketing companies

"Betty, I know I have been unsuccessful in several different network marketing companies. I take responsibility for not fully committing. I am sick and tired of flaking out and not making it happen. I found a new network marketing company that I am excited about. This one is different. I know everyone says theirs is different. So do this. Take a look; if it makes sense, then great. Suppose it doesn't, no worries.

THE ULTIMATE SCRIPT BOOK

My goal is to do whatever it takes to (insert goal or goals) within one year. I know everything worthwhile is harder than we think it will be. It may take 2 or 3 years, but I will do whatever it takes."

"I know you have been watching me over the last several years change to several different companies as I have tried to be successful. This is hard to admit, but honestly, I haven`t been fully committed in the past. That`s a tough pill to swallow! But I found a new company that I am excited about, and already it makes more sense and aligns with everything I want. My goal is to do whatever it takes to succeed with this business. I am ready to do the hard work and stay accountable to making this successful?"

The script first interaction after you haven't spoken to someone in years

"Hey, Rob. I am so excited to catch up with you. I want to be direct. I have a new business venture (you can use whatever term you want instead of the business venture) that I want to talk to you about but let`s catch up first. When works best, beginning of the week or end of the week?" (when they respond-GREAT Morning or afternoon? Afternoon, ok awesome I have (insert two options IE 1 or 3) They respond-3pm. Excellent! I can`t wait to catch up and get your opinion on this.

Lessons from the scripts.

"I want to apologize for not connecting sooner #momlife Didn`t want you to think I had forgotten about you. How have you been?

"You`ve been on my mind today, and I can`t stop thinking about how this $500 bonus has helped so many people and how it could help you and your family, too. Other than fear, what`s stopping you from getting started?"

FIRST INTERACTIONS AND SIMPLE INVITES

Lessons from the scripts from first interactions-

Don't forget to apply your own words. The principle is that I was very direct, which I am sure most people would appreciate. I also followed it with being a good human because I care about people and want to catch up with long-lost friends. Yes, it is that simple.

Leonardo DaVinci said it best.
"Simplicity is the ultimate sophistication."

You can also insert anything about your products if you are looking for a customer rather than a distributor. If Jared had used this to approach me, I would have known exactly what type of conversation we would be having. People don't say this because they are afraid they will get rejected. If Jared had sent me this message, I would have STILL been a YES! I would have been thrilled to catch up and hear all about what he had going on with his new business.

Use the principle of this script, and you will have much more confidence to reach out to people you haven't spoken to in years.

Let's shift your mindset real quick. Most network marketers feel like they are givers but are worried about being perceived as takers. Due to this FEAR, they stop approaching people they know. They are scared to death of the mother of all fears! The fear of judgment. If you haven't already, grab my book, *The Game of Conquering* at www.thegameofconquering.com It hits hard on everything to do with your mindset. Mindset will eat skills and systems for breakfast. You will want to check that book out, but to give you a quick solution right here, you have to SHIFT your perspective about how you are thinking about your opportunity and offer. If I was bleeding and you had a bandaid, would you feel shy about offering it to me? NO! You would come right over and say, "Hey Rob, looks like you are bleeding; I have a bandaid if you want to use it." Whether I said yes or no would be irrelevant to you. Start to shift your thinking around making offers to help people!

THE INVITES

We have shared some basic scripts to make the first interaction and simple invites when connecting with people. Now it's time to start making a specific invite and offer to try a product, learn more information, or come to an event. Use the scripts below to create edification and credibility with people as you move to the next conversation with people.

Your goal is to only SELL ONE THING. This is CRUCIAL. If you ask someone to follow you, sign up, watch a video, and subscribe to your YOUTUBE channel, you have overwhelmed the offer. We hate to break it to you, but the more you ask people to do, the less they will do. You have to ask people to do one thing at a time. This is known as a call to action. You are essentially moving through the next step of the process. You are selling them by taking a look and using whatever tools your company and team use. You sell them by checking out a webinar, FB group, or video. If your invite becomes a full-on pitch, you are in trouble. You are the preview to the movie. You are not the movie, so remember to focus on ONE offer at a time.

The scripts to invite to 3 way or group chat

People need to hear another voice to validate what they hope to be true. Edification gives QUICK credibility and connection to the prospect and the leader(s) you include. Edifying is just quickly building up someone else in a truthful way. Here are a few example of edifying in a simple way.

3rd party validation or, in other words, just another voice to build the credibility mentioned earlier. These options, one product, and one business example create a few things: Excitement, 3rd party validation, and the opportunity to serve this prospect together! It's an opportunity for the upline to be introduced and the prospect to quickly learn how to use this tool to enroll more customers and reps quickly.

Scheduling a call where everyone is available can be difficult and frustrating with people having busy lives. A group chat in place of a three-way call allows each person to respond when available and takes one obstacle (connecting everyone at the same time) away. A group chat is typically a chat created on FB messenger but could be created via regular text, WhatsApp telegram, etc.

The reasons why I strongly prefer a group chat are:

1 - Success loves speed. You don't need to coordinate times with the prospect and the leader or whoever does the 3rd party validation.

2 - It is less intrusive, which creates even more duplication.

3 - You can go back to chats to see the exact conversation you had.

It is important to remember that edifying goes both ways. You need to CONNECT the two in the chat, so do NOT forget to edify your prospect as well.

The scripts for inviting to meet a third party

"Linda, this is Mary. Mary is one of my business besties! She is also a homeschool momma running a multi-million dollar business around her busy family."

Mary, this is Linda. Linda is a fellow homeschool mom, her husband is in the military and she is looking to add an additional income, but isn't sure she has the time it takes to be successful. She has checked

THE ULTIMATE SCRIPT BOOK

out (whatever tool your prospect viewed/encountered) and is interested in hearing how she can work this into her busy momlife. Linda, could you share some examples of how you manage to make it all work?

"_____, I want to introduce you to Joanna. Joanna has been using the products for six months and has an incredible story on how they have helped her tremendously."

"_____, I want to introduce you to one of my business partners. John has been a part of our business for the last seven months and made his money back from his initial investment within four weeks following our system."

"_____, I want to introduce you to Sam, who is a business partner of mine. Sam has consistently made six figures a year for the last four years. She is a good friend and has had a ton of success following our system. I am excited to have you both chat."

"Hey _____, I added my friend John to this group chat. John is a good friend who has had an incredible experience with the (fill in the product name or just say business depending on if this is a business or product approach)."

"Hey _____! I want to introduce you to my good friend Sam. Sam first introduced me to these products that have helped me achieve _____, and we're excited to see how they can best help you too! We'd love to help answer any questions you may have before getting started with us."

"Hi Sam, Mary has looked at _____and is interested in learning more about _____. Mary, Sam is here to help answer that question you had about _____."

"Hey _____, as promised, I wanted to introduce you to my good friend Sally who is brilliant when it comes to building a business online. You recently shared with me about wanting to figure out a way to make some extra money from home, so I thought it would be great to connect you with us here to help answer any questions you may have about what we are up to. You`ve seen my success over the last few months, and we`re excited to see how we can best help you!"

"Hi_____I wanted to introduce you to my friend Sally who is an expert in (product). You recently shared with me that you were having issues with_____and I thought it would be great to connect you here so that _____could answer any questions for you. You know how much success I have had with that same issue these past months, and _____was a major part of helping me achieve that. They are here to help!"

The Scripts to invite to receive a sample or more information

Occasionally, people are ready to go and want to jump right in! Most often, they want to learn more. This can be done through samples and receiving more information through three-way messages or events. You can also send people links to videos to watch, company and product information, or even talk to someone else that has used the product or started in the business recently. Here are a couple of different ways you can invite someone who would like more information.

"Hi_____Thanks for being open to learning more about_____. I think you will like the benefits that this can offer you. To send this to you, I am going to need your address. Would you mind sending it to me?"

"Hey_____I wanted to pop in and send you that link I promised you. Go ahead and read everything, and I will message you tomorrow to see if you have any questions."

"Thanks for taking the time to learn more about_____. I remember when I first started that I wanted to talk to a couple more people too. I have included a couple of my friends` names and numbers that you can reach out to. I texted them, and they are excited to chat with you. Are you open to me following up with you after chatting with them?"

The Scripts to invite to business launch and events

People love to support others who are doing something new. We often miss a HUGE opportunity to have people support us when we don`t invite them to celebrate with us in our new business venture. As you think about inviting people to learn more about your new business, you want to focus on two things. First, share the information about the new business; second, invite them to come and learn more and support you.

Think about how you want to tell people about your business launch. If I were starting a new business, I would tell people, "I am launching a new business." If that`s not the phrase you would use, that`s ok. I suggest taking the script and writing it in your own words, remembering the principle of being authentic and utilizing the framework.

"Would you do me a favor? I just started selling _____ and looking for a few friends who are willing to try out the products for a month. It is only _____. If they help you, great! If not, there is no need to ever order them again, but I think you will love them. Is that ok?"

"Hi_____. I have been using _____ had amazing results, so I decided to launch my own business and help others like me. Would you or someone you know be willing to try a couple of items and give me your honest feedback?"

FIRST INTERACTIONS AND SIMPLE INVITES

"Hey_____,hope you're doing well. You may or may not have seen that I recently started my own online business. Now I know you probably have zero interest in looking at the business side, but based on what I've seen you post/talk about recently, I feel you may benefit greatly from the products! Are you open to taking a look at how they might help you? If not, no worries."

Hey, _____! Find something you can talk about to catch up. Check out their FB profile real quickly to find something to talk about. For example." How was your trip? What's new in your world? How is your family? How was _____?"

"I just joined a Facebook community focused on health with one of the leading products being focused on (SELL BENEFIT), and I love it! This is a positive group that already has over _____ members. Since I started using_____, I have had less pain in my back (insert anything this product has done for you) so far on these products (Or share a testimonial of a friend: "I'm excited to start using some of the products. My friend has already _____). No pressure either way! Let me know if you'd like to check it out, and I'll add you."

"Hey_____! I wanted to catch up with you. I just saw that you had been_____. That looks amazing. I have been busy lately! I found a way to make money by using my phone. OMG, you have to see this ... I can add you to a private Facebook community with over _____ members that you must check out. I'm already experiencing success (share your results and your reason. If you haven't had success yet, share the excitement of your goals)."

"I would love to add you to this Facebook group where you can learn more about the incredible products we offer and how you can use them."

"I am launching a new business to help (insert why you started here. IE to help pay for my student loans or pay for a family trip to see the family, etc.) Would you be willing to help me with my training and show up and ask questions? The more you ask, the more it helps me learn how to answer other people's questions. I don't know if they ask the same thing. Can I count on you for your support?"

If they say yes, say: "THANK YOU SO MUCH!! I knew I could count on you :) Here is the link for the event (send them the link to the event) and say: "I will send you a reminder in the morning to confirm. I know Facebook doesn't always show everyone notifications, so make sure to select "GOING." Also, if open to it, feel free to invite a few friends you feel wouldn't mind having a chance to win some cool giveaways!"

"I am getting ready to launch one of the biggest businesses in our lifetime, and you were one of the first people that came to mind because I know I could count on you for your support. This may or may not be for you; I promise I wouldn't waste your time. If you're not interested, I'll never bother you again, but I think you may, or you might know someone that is. I don't have all of the details, but I have partnered with a successful mentor to help me get started. Your support would mean the world to me. Are you available at (insert date/time) to show up and ask questions to help me with my training?"

"I know that we discussed how much you love (insert subject). I am hosting an event this weekend at (insert date and time), and we will be talking about that very thing. It would be awesome to have you join us, and I promise you will get all of your questions answered."

"Hey, I know exactly what you are doing this weekend! I'm having an event with some of my friends. I started doing a business that looks like it can help many people, and we can make some money. Can I count you in?"

Lessons from the Invite

Invites are here to benefit you and the person you are speaking with. They help you get the information to them. The person gets an invite to an opportunity they may have never had before. Start thinking of the invite as a win/win for both of you. The biggest obstacle for people is that they see the invite as the person doing them a favor. Remember, this is a benefit for BOTH of you. When making the invite, it has to be authentic to you if this feels too scripted or robotic.

Here is a quick example of how one of my clients adjusted this script to be authentic to her voice and style. One of my clients was launching a new business, and she sent out invites to come and celebrate at an online business bash. Once people said YES to coming, she sent this message to people she knew. "THANK YOU! You are a goddess! Here is the link to get you into this highly exclusive member-only group. Because you are with me, you are instantly a member. I will text you the day of to remind you to come and party with me. Ensure to RSVP and hit the "going" button when it pops up. Ain`t no real party unless you are there!"

Now, this script works for HER. Can you imagine if I tried to send this script out?! My client took the principle and adjusted the script to fit her authentic personality. She has massive success because everyone knows she is fun-loving and a riot to be around. Everyone wants to come and party with her online AND in person.

THE ULTIMATE SCRIPT BOOK

SECTION 3

FOLLOW-UP

You have likely heard the phrase, "The fortune is in the follow-up," but what does it mean?." Rob had eleven different network marketing companies approach him before saying yes. The biggest reason he said no to all of them was the lack of follow-up. People would pitch and disappear. Don`t be that person! Remember, NONE of these scripts will be successful without follow-up. Everyone asks, "How soon should I follow up?" A good rule of thumb is, if someone is directly messaging you back, you should check it and respond within 24 hours. People change their minds quickly. If they have said yes to the opportunity, and you wait three days to follow up, they have already moved on with their lives and may have forgotten the yes already. Not to mention, their excitement has likely dwindled. Quick follow-up is one of the most significant ways to create success in your business.

One thing that holds many people back from following up is when they get an objection. Objections aren`t bad and should not dissuade you from following up. When someone gives you an objection, look at it positively because they provide the problem they need to solve before saying yes. The follow-up begins straight from the last conversation. You should always set up your next time to connect. You may or may not have heard this acronym before-BAMFAM. Book A Meeting From A Meeting. Put it in the calendar and schedule it out, or it is doubtful it will happen. Every interaction you have, should have a follow up scheduled afterwords.

Let's say that someone wants to buy a product from you. There will need to be a follow-up! You will have to send a product link, answer questions, etc. There is not ONE SINGLE interaction that doesn't have a follow-up that goes along with it. Even the person that is a "No" will get a follow-up. The timing of the follow-up matters, and we want to be clear that you will need to set up your follow-up system. Coach Fryer will share his follow-up system that led to his and his client's success in the business. This system is key to tracking and remembering where you are in your follow-up process with every prospect. This section is MASSIVE because we believe so much in follow-up. We didn't want to leave anything out. We are so passionate about follow-up that Coach has created a follow-up system that even helps with the timing of each follow-up.

Coach Fryer's 1-3-7 formula for follow-up

The 1-3-7 follow-up formula has been used by tens of thousands of network marketers worldwide. It's increased their overall conversions rate by 200% and has saved our clients a TON of time learning the exact process of following up with everyone.

When I, Coach, started network marketing, I was crazy busy! I was not only trying to build a business, but I was also coaching high-level athletes in baseball. As a former professional baseball player, I was always in high demand! I found it hard to remember when and how long to follow up with people in my network marketing business. That is when I created the 1-3-7 formula. This cut out the guesswork with follow-ups and made it easy to follow even with a busy life. I know that many of you are in that same position. You may be starting your network marketing business while still having a full-time job. Don`t let that become your excuse. You can do this! Below is the formula and details about how to use it to create momentum and an actual system for following up with people.

1-Day Follow-Up:

- Mention previous conversation
- Don`t assume the worst; give them the benefit of the doubt (maybe they just got busy or sidetracked)
- "Hey _____, hope you`re having a great day! I`d love to help answer any more questions you may have about _____ (insert problem discussed). How else can I best help?" :)

3-Day Follow Up:

- No mention of the previous conversation
- View as 'touching point.`
- "Thought I would stop by real quick ____(insert name) and say that I hope you are having a great day/week! Anything fun planned for the weekend?" :)

7-Day Follow-Up:

- Time to create URGENCY
- Insert FOMO

"Hey _____! I wanted to circle back around one last time before crossing you off my follow-up list. A few days ago, you shared how you were struggling with _____(insert their problem). I'm excited to see how I can help you take that next step in (insert solution/feeling/outcome)!"

The 1-3-7 follow-up script has now been used by tens of thousands of network marketers, helped them ACCELERATE the number of new signups, and reduced the overall 'wait-time` of the prospect being ready.

It's true; the FORTUNE in network marketing truly is in the follow-up! As we mentioned before, you never stop following up. But you may start to put some time in between the follow-ups. Clients come to us and say, "I have done all the follow-ups and haven't got this person to sign up in two months!" That's ok. Not everyone will, but you can still put them on a list to follow up every six months, or maybe every year. We don't want to be like Rob's long-lost friend, who suddenly popped up when he needed something. Stay connected once you make the connection. The following are great scripts to follow up in several different situations.

The scripts for 24-hour follow-up with a stranger

"Hey _____, it was great to connect with you last night at (insert event). It was great to meet someone with a passion for a business like I do. I wondered if you would be open to hearing more about what we talked about last night?"

"It was so great to meet you, and thanks for following me on (insert social platform). I know that you and I share a love for business, and I couldn't stop thinking about creating more business for both of us. Would you be open to checking out (insert business or product)? I have loved being involved, and I think you would too."

"So excited that I got to connect with you. We had so much in common that I am pretty surprised we hadn`t met before this. Since we have so much in common, I was wondering if you would be open to hearing more about_____. I have loved it, and I think you may too."

"So fun to connect with you at _____. Hopefully, we can stay connected and get to know each other better. Would you be open to meeting up and getting to know each other better?"

"HEY! I found you on here! I always love meeting people in person and being able to connect here too. I loved to see how much you love (Insert something on their feed). Let`s get together soon. Is there a day/time that works for you?"

The scripts for 24-hour follow-up with people you know

"Ever since we spoke yesterday, I can`t stop thinking about what you said. I hate knowing people are dealing with _____. Would you be open to passing my info or connecting me to those struggling people? I`ve seen such incredible improvements I`d hate to know they could feel better like I am."

"I can`t stop thinking about what you said yesterday. I hate knowing you are dealing with _____. Would you be open to checking out what I have been using to get my _____? I`ve seen such incredible improvements myself. I`d hate to know they could feel better like I am."

"I appreciate you checking this out. I know that your time is valuable, and I want to ensure I am not wasting your time. I wanted to see what you thought about (insert invite) from yesterday. If you are willing, we can get on the phone, and I can give you more details. It would only take a 30-minute phone call. I know how busy you are. What do you think?"

"_____, I know you are crazy busy, so I want to thank you for making time to connect. Looking forward to chatting at seven tonight."

"I want to apologize for not connecting sooner #momlife Didn't want you to think I'd forgotten about you. How have you been?"

"Before I forget, I know you wanted to get started with the (insert product) to help you (insert problem). When did you think you'd like to give it a try?"

"Hi____ :) Not one to push because it's not my style; I know you were interested in giving (insert Product) a try. I didn't want you to think I had forgotten about you (#momlife lol). When did you think you'd like to get started?"

"Did that link work ok for you? I never like to assume technology works."

"It was great to meet you today at _____! If you have any questions, I'd be honored to assist. Feel free to check out the site or join the VIP testimonial group _____."

"So sorry I missed your birthday! How did you spend your special day?"

"Happy belated Birthday! What is one thing you are most looking forward to next year?"

"I bet you thought I forgot your birthday yesterday. WRONG! I just wanted to be special and tell you happy birthday today."

"Happy birthday! What is one thing you want to accomplish this next year around the sun?"

"Happiest of birthdays to you. What are you looking forward to today?"

FOLLOW-UP

The Scripts for Product Sample Follow up

Setting the right expectation BEFORE you send out any samples is vital for samples turning into future customers! Before sending any out, be sure they agree to a few things:

"Hey there _____. How are you? I had a sec, and I recall at one point you had expressed interest in wanting to improve your health (have more energy, sleep better, live longer, make some money, etc.). We`ve launched a new product and are getting great feedback from its results. I`ve got limited samples and was curious if I shared one with you. Would you try it and give me your feedback? If not, then no worries. I just wanted to give you a chance before I run out."

"Hi_____Thanks for being open to receiving a sample of the product. I wanted to let you know what to expect. I have sent out the sample, and you should receive it in the next couple of days. Let me know when you get it."

"Great to hear you got your sample safe and sound! Have you had a chance to open them up? Are there any questions I can answer for you?"

"Bummer you haven`t gotten your sample yet. The post office can be so tricky lately. I hope they haven`t gotten lost. Will you do me a favor and let me know when you receive them?"

"I would love to hear what your experience has been. What has been your feeling about using the product?"

"Thank you so much for reaching out and getting a sample of the product. Would you be open to sharing your personal story using the product?"

"Thanks for hopping on the live tonight! Did you have any questions or learn something new?"

I am so excited to hear how you love it! Are you thinking of starting as a customer or becoming an affiliate and sharing with friends?"

"Before I forget, I know you wanted to get started with the (insert product) to help you (insert problem). When did you think you'd like to give it a try?"

"Not one to push because it's not my style; I know you were interested in giving (insert Product) a try. I didn't want you to think I had forgotten about you (#momlife lol). When did you think you'd like to get started?"

The Scripts on how to ask for a referral

Referrals can be a HUGE part of your business if you use them correctly. Think of it like this...if you have an existing LOYAL customer that refers you to a new customer, it probably took little to NO effort on your part. You can create MORE business by getting more direct referrals. Here are a few thoughts and a script to help start this conversation with existing customers. Customers ALWAYS make the best builders because it started with a result in the product, making their conviction to share even GREATER!

- Adding new customers each month via referral can help increase residual checks by several hundred dollars a month.

- Treating your existing customers like GOLD will only increase the level of trust and their willingness to share with others (for free).

- Create a couple of SIMPLE curiosity posts your existing customers could post on their wall to potentially help you generate a few referral customers. Referral posts are a great way to upgrade a happy customer to a happy team member.

FOLLOW-UP

"Hey _____(insert name)! I first just wanted to thank you for being such a loyal customer over the last 6-months. Seeing you overcome (insert their original pain/problem here) in such a short time has been amazing. I was curious, do you by chance know of anyone else struggling with (insert hat pain again here) that you feel we could help? If not, no biggie."

"Hey _____(insert name), hope you and the family are doing well. First of all, I just want to thank you for being such a loyal customer. Seeing your results (insert SPECIFIC result they have had) has been incredible and got me thinking. Do you by chance know of anyone else who could also benefit from what you are experiencing?"

"Hey _____(insert your customer name)! Isn`t this exciting? Betsy is excited to start the products! Now there`s one of two ways we can help her. I can enroll her as my customer, and I would get the kickback commission, about $15. Or option 2, we can help get YOU upgraded now, and YOU enroll her. You get the commission now, and every time she orders in the future. Which would you prefer?"

The scripts for Vendor Event Follow Up

"It was great to meet you today at _____! If you have any questions, I`d be honored to assist. Feel free to check out the site or join the VIP testimonial group _____."

"Congratulations _____, you were selected as the winner from the (insert company name) booth at (name the event)!!! Could you please send me your address and I will get that out to you ASAP? Thanks and congrats again!!"

"Just wanted to let you know that you were the winner selected for (insert prize) at the (company name) booth from the (insert event).

53

THE ULTIMATE SCRIPT BOOK

Congratulations! I also wanted to let you know as a winner, you have the opportunity to (have a girl`s night/pamper party, etc.) for you and up to 5 friends. We can do it at the beginning of the week or the end of the week. When is the best time that works for you?" (NOTE: this is for a party plan model).

"Hi_____we met at the (insert event). I wanted to reach out because I have a gift for you. I could tell you were interested in _____, and so I wanted to give you a chance to try it."

The scripts for FB or Social Platform Live EVENT follow-up

"Thanks so much for tuning in tonight! It means a lot that you were able to attend. Did you learn anything new or have any questions I could answer for you?"

Hey Chantel, it`s Greg. Did I catch you at a good time?..... I am touching base with you because we`re launching new products next week and expanding to more countries. I hate to see you miss out on pioneering the forefront with this fast and trending global movement. Do you have any other questions I can answer for you, or are you ready to get started?"

"So great to see you on the live today. It is always so awesome to be able to educate people about _____. I wanted to follow up with you and see if you were open to trying out_____. Because you were on the live, I am offering a free sample to anyone who would like to test it out. Is that something you would be interested in?"

"Thanks for checking out the live today. It was so great to see your name pop up. It`s nice to see a familiar name! I am following up with everyone on the live and wanted to know if you are open to learning more about_____."

FOLLOW-UP

The scripts when someone asks for more information

"I'd be honored to-is there something specific I can answer for you?"

"Is there something specific you are looking to use it for?"

"That's great that you are interested in giving it a try. I would be happy to give you a sample and talk with you about its benefits. I also love to encourage anyone interested in doing their research and figuring out what works best for them. If this is it, I am happy to help get you started."

"I have the perfect group that you should join. It has a bunch of testimonials from people going through the same thing as you. Would you like to check it out?"

"If you are interested in learning more, I can send you a link to join a FB group where my group has posted several research articles, testimonials, and helpful info. I can tag you in a couple of posts to get you the exact info you are looking for."

"If you have any other questions, I would love to answer them. I don't want to leave you hanging."

"What are you using right now to help you with _____?"

"What seems to be the biggest challenge you're having with the _____product you are currently using, and how much do you typically spend each month on that product?"

"It can be a real challenge to feel like you have tried several things, and they haven't worked as you hoped. If you would like, I can show you why this product is different and share with you some testimonials from people that have tried it and had the success you are looking to achieve."

"Thanks for agreeing to look at the information. I am looking forward to hearing what you liked best. Below are the steps to check out some more information. Use this link and watch a five-minute video to get more information.

"I just wanted to follow up with you. Do you have any questions after watching the video? I would love to hop on a call with you and my business partner _____. She has been in this industry for years and knows all of the answers that can help get you started."

"Thanks for hopping on the live tonight! Did you have any questions or learn something new?"

"I am so excited to hear how you love it! Are you thinking of starting as a customer or becoming a (rep/affiliate/consultant etc.) and sharing with friends?"

"You`ve been on my mind, and I didn`t want you to think I forgot about you. Were you ready to give (product) a try for (insert ailment)? *OR talk about what you've noticed in their feed- generally, they will bring it up. If not, you can say,* "before I forget, Were you ready to give (product) a try for (insert ailment)?"

"Hey_____I was thinking about you today. My company is having a flash sale for today only. I knew that we had talked about how you were interested a while back. Right now is a great time to give it a try at a huge discount. Would you like me to send you some info?"

"My team has an awesome promo on that product you were interested in. Would you be open to getting some more info about it? The promo ends tomorrow."

"I know you messaged me a while back about trying (product) to help with your (insert problem). Are you still interested in giving it a try? I hate knowing you're dealing with that."

"I know this is random, but every time you pop up on my newsfeed, I can't get out of my head how awesome you'd be doing what I do, especially being on social media as much as you are, lol. Would you be interested in learning how to make money on the side using social media in your spare time?"

"Hey (insert name), congratulations on (an event that happened last year). It has been great to follow along with your life on (insert social platform). This year has been great for me. The business that we talked about has been awesome. It keeps growing! I would love to connect and hear about what you have been up to. Is that something you are open to?"

The Scripts for the awkward follow-up when you get ghosted

If you haven't been ghosted yet, you haven't been in network marketing long enough. The definition of being ghosted is when someone just stops communicating with you. You don't know if they have no interest or if something happened in their life. It can feel worse if you have been ghosted by someone you know because you don't want it to be awkward the next time you see them. Don't worry; we've got you covered. Here are some scripts you can use if someone has stopped communicating with you.

"Hey _____, I had not heard back, so I wanted to make sure you are ok? <3 Hope you are well!"

Hi there! Checking to make sure you are alright since I had not heard from you <3 Everything ok?

"I know you are very busy. I never want you to feel like I am pestering you. I know this _____ could be a blessing in your life. What do you think?"

"Hey _____, I know how busy you have been with your two littles at home and working full time. You are superwoman! I understand and don't want you to feel like I am bugging you about joining this group. I just wanted to follow up and tell you that I am always here to talk about this opportunity."

Other ideas to bump the chat

GIFS-Often a silly gif will lighten the mood. Pick 1 or 2 funny ones (BUELLER for example) and a quick comment of are you still there lol?

If this is not your personality, choose another approach.

PRO TIP: Changing the color of the chat or emoji in the chat bumps the message for the other person so it looks like you messaged them again. If you pick a type of emoji or color to help you visually remember a key point of your chat (maybe a money bag for business or a water droplet for something that they wanted to try that goes in water).

Lessons to learn from the follow-up

No one wants to be a number. People like to connect with others and feel like others genuinely care about them. Follow-up is all about caring enough to reach out and connect with others. Jim Rohn said, "service to many leads to greatness." The ultimate service to others is not leaving them out or forgetting about them. Continue to follow up regardless of what they say at the moment. It doesn't have to be creepy or have a plan. It can be about caring for others and reaching out to see how they are doing, congratulate them, mourn with them, and be a good human. We say that follow-up is forever because you never know when people's lives will change and when they may seriously start to consider a different product or business. Be someone that they can look to and that they remember. Following up consistently keeps you top of mind and helps people know that you genuinely care.

THE ULTIMATE SCRIPT BOOK

SECTION 4

OBJECTIONS

We have all been in the position of facing objections when it comes to enrolling or even getting people to look at the product or business. These are objections where scripts work incredibly well. Sometimes when the prospect has heard the offer, and when you finally get to the "let's get started," they hesitate or back out. We have made a list of the most significant objections that we have both heard over and over again in network marketing. We would love to hear the objections you get in your business. Post on social media and tag us @robsperry and @coachfryer with the #biggestobjections. Below are the scripts that we have come up with for handling the top objections in the industry. In this section, we have given you scripts for the biggest objections that everyone faces in network marketing.

The scripts for the objection of no money

Make sure that when people give you the objection of "no money" that you aren't letting your own beliefs about money get in the way.

I see people falter when someone says they don't have money because they believe them or they doubt if the person can really make their money back. Don't do this! People spend their money countless different ways and you don't get to decide what that looks like. And, if you truly believe in the product and the offer, you will believe that anyone can make money doing this business, or get the results that the product is offering. Don't let money objections get in the way

"I don't know many people that start this business because they have extra money. lol, they do it because they NEED it! :) I didn't have the money either. I finally got creative and figured out a way to get it. I put it on a credit card, and I have had people sell old things, babysit, clean houses, borrow, use a credit card; you just have to be creative. And you have to decide how much an extra $500 would help your family a month. Some have also asked friends or family to borrow the money until their products come in and sell to pay them back. Which of these things would be something you'd be willing to do?"

"If I could show you how to turn your startup into (insert desired income) in the next 30-90 days, would this be something you would like to try?

"That's not a problem, and I'm not asking you to buy anything. Once you review the info, we can go from there and see if you are interested."

"If you could make your money back in the next thirty days, would this opportunity be something you would like to start?"

"I get it. This is the biggest struggle that people face when starting something new. If I could help you get creative and figure out how to get started, would you be open to getting started?"

The scripts for the objection of no time

Time is a construct that we all live by. There is not one person that has "no time." We ALL have time. In fact, we all have the exact same amount of time. People are deciding how to use that time, but the "no time" excuse has never sat well with either one of us. Don`t let this objection fool you into believing that there are people out there with no time.

"_____, I know how busy you are based on what you have told me. I run 99% of my business on social media and teach my team to do the same. Are you coachable and willing to learn how to use social media as a tool to earn the income you desire?"

"One of the best parts about this industry and business is that we believe in time freedom. If I could teach you how to be successful in this business, investing four hours a week, would you be open to learning more?"

"Time is something that we all wish we had more of. If I could show you exactly how to gain more time and create more wealth, would you be open to hearing more about the solution?"

The scripts for the objection of "I don't know enough people"

When anyone comes to us and says that they don`t know enough people, both of use want to say something like, "sounds like a good reason to get into network marketing!" There is no requirement for how many people you need to know in order to be in network marketing.

"You don`t need to-I Didn`t know a single person on our team when they got started! You can reach people worldwide with social media as I have, and I will teach you how! As a top leader in this industry, I pride myself on helping my team be successful. Are you coachable and willing to learn?"

"One of the best parts about this business is that you can start small. You don't need to know a lot of people to make an impact and start earning money. If you are open to learning, I can teach you how to start this business exactly where you are at today."

"We all start where we are in this business. I have seen people become successful and know LESS people than you do. If you are willing, I can teach you how to meet people. You just have to be open to doing it."

The scripts for the objection of needing to think about it:

"_____That tells me I didn't answer something you needed more info on. What will you be thinking about? What other questions do you think may need to be answered?"

"I understand that you want to take some time to think this over. Why don't you take the pillow test tonight and we can connect tomorrow?"

The scripts for the objection of needing to talk to someone else

Most of use have someone that we run by big events or purchases in our lives. That's great! But often people use the excuse that they need to talk to someone else. Realize that this may be an excuse, or it may be a legitmate thing for some. Use these scripts to help you figure out what is really going on.

"Can I ask you something? If you decided to go to college, would you talk to a college graduate or a dropout? I just want you to make sure whomever you ask advice from, that you would be willing to switch places with them because you are the only one that can determine if you will be successful as a graduate or fail to try and never get started."

"I understand that you want to talk to _____ before you get started. What do you think they are going to say about you wanting to try this product? Are there any questions that you think I can answer right now to help you have the conversation?"

"If you think about it all after we finish, you should at least give it a try because, for your sake, in a few weeks, I don't want you to wonder, "what if?"

(need to talk to spouse)

"I understand. I would love it if we could get together with all of us so that I can answer any questions that both of you have."

"Hi _____, this is (insert name) with (company name), how are you? Great! I was just calling to answer any questions you may have after speaking with your spouse. Did you think about what we talked about at all or have any other questions I can answer for you?"

The scripts for the objection of pyramid scheme

People get so nervous that someone will call network marketing a pyramid scheme. There is no reason to get defensive on any objection, even if they bring up a pyramid scheme. There is such a vast difference between responding to someone vs. reacting to someone. There is no reason to react to any objection that comes up. The best thing you can do is listen to what the person is saying and respond to the objection. Don't take anything personally.

Our good friend Simon Chan from MLM Nation says the following. He says three different aspects to the objection about this business being a pyramid scheme. You must ask the prospect to clarify what he means in all three instances.

You don't know their true meaning yet, so don't jump to conclusions. Many people don't mean any harm by saying it is a pyramid scheme. I have found that they say you can build a team and make money from building a team of customers and business builders. Always start with asking questions upon questions in a non-defensive way!

"Tell me_____what makes you think that network marketing is a pyramid scheme?"

"What does a pyramid scheme mean to you? What about this business makes you think that is how our business is run?"

"It sounds like you have heard a lot about pyramid schemes. How many people do you know with network marketing businesses?"

"This is not a pyramid scheme. Pyramid schemes are illegal, and I would never get you to do something like that. Now, would you be interested to learn more about what I have to share with you?"

"The best part of our business is that you can start at the bottom and make more money than the people at the top. At my job, I could never earn more money than my boss, and that's why I am so excited and love this business so much. Would you be interested to learn more about how this works?"

The lesson to learn from handling objections

Handling objections is all about your listening skills. You need to hear what people are saying and not take it personally. Most people get so worked up about hearing someone give them an objection. That is part of the sales process. Your job is to listen, let the person know that you hear them and what they are saying, ask any follow-up questions, and then answer the objection directly. People always have to choose to say no, but when you can remember your goal when answering objections, it will help you feel confident about what you are saying and how you are saying it.

See this as an opportunity to educate! From our personal experience and the thousands of clients we collectively have, we know that network marketing is one of the most successful business models. In 2021 it was estimated that the network marketing industry did $325 billion combined. When people ask about pyramid schemes or anything like that, rest assured that you have stats and 100 years of history on your side. There is no reason to get defensive or hurt by someone else's lack of knowledge.

SECTION 5

CLOSING PROSPECTS

We have both got questions from our clients about closing a deal. Rob once got a frantic message on Instagram from someone who had just started network marketing. It said, "Rob, you have got to help me out! I have people that want to sign up, but what do I say??? HELP! My sponsor told me what to say to get people jazzed about the product, but she never told me what to say after that!"

We both wish we all had the problem of too many people wanting our product and to build in this business! But honestly, we have both seen that this step gets skipped a lot. Many sponsors believe that it will be easy to close the deal and either get them the products or get them started in the business once someone is interested. That is not always the case. We wanted to include some scripts to help you close. Please remember that the close will depend on what people want and what you offer. Here are some of the BEST closing scripts in the profession:

The scripts for closing

"Hey _____. Circling back around one last time before crossing you off my flist. Are you still looking for help (insert their problem here), or have you already found a solution?"

"Hey _____! It was great chatting with you the other day, and I was surprised to learn of (their problem here). I shared a bit about what may help and what's helping me. On a scale of 1-10, how open are you to trying it out?"

"Hi_____. I am here to help you. Let's get you started with (insert product or business) to get you the results you have been looking for."

"Let's get you signed up and added to my team FaceBook group. I want to help you get the result you are after as soon as possible."

"Great! I am excited to be working with you. The next step is to____."

"On a scale of 1-10, what is your interest level in getting started today?"

"Is there ANY reason why we couldn't get you started today?"

"Are there any questions I can answer before you get started?"

Lessons from closing

Once you have someone interested in buying a product or starting with the business, the main thing that you need to focus on is the NEXT STEP. Don't get too caught up in the future and what it will look like. Focus on the next step that this person needs to do to move them forward with the business. We see people get tripped up trying to overcomplicate the process. Ask yourself, "What is the next step this person needs to know?" Once you can figure that out, you can make the next contact with them.

We always say that fortune is in the follow-up. One of the biggest mistakes people make is not making the next follow-up.

When Rob shared some of these scripts with the person that had a new customer, she was underwhelmed. "Is that it?" she asked. YES! Don`t overcomplicate it. Sometimes the easy scripts are the ones that convert and help your customers and business builders the most. Let it be simple. Anyone can overcomplicate it; it takes a genius to keep it simple.

THE ULTIMATE SCRIPT BOOK

SECTION 6

SOCIAL MEDIA SCRIPTS

We wanted to give social media its own section because, let's be honest, it is its own beast. When it comes to social media, you have to show up differently than you do in person or even over text or phone. Social media has become the top place where people build their online businesses, and network marketing is no exception. Each social platform has strengths and weaknesses, and there isn't one "best" platform to post and use. It does depend on who your audience is and where you like to show up. We want to mention a couple of social media platforms to use and why they would be a benefit to you.

LinkedIn is the social platform that boasts being "The largest professional network on the internet." LinkedIn has some massive strengths but some vast annoyances. The most significant difference between LinkedIn and every other platform is that people are more direct on LinkedIn. Because it is a professional network, people are willing to dive right in with business opportunities and offers. This means that you will receive more SPAM-type messages than any other platform. I always talk about how your weaknesses can be your strengths, and that goes for LinkedIn and direct messages.

Instagram is a great place if you like to interact through pictures, captions, stories, and short videos. We have seen Instagram take off with business these past several years.

Tik Tok is a great platform if you love making videos and staying very consistent with posting. This is a perfect place if you have information to share in a fun way.

And of course, there is the OG...the original social platform that has withstood the test of time; Facebook. Facebook is a great platform that combines all of the above features into one place. It also has one of our favorite features; groups. This was a quick overview, and if you want to learn more we suggest doing some research on the platforms yourself.

It is best to pick a platform and focus on it. Once you have become great at one platform, you should look into expanding into other platforms. The scripts that I will share here are customized for LinkedIn but can be used on any platform you feel comfortable with.

Regardless of what platform you decide to start with or continue to use, remember that we both don't recommend dropping an offer in the first message. That being said, we will break our own rule here and say that there are some platforms like LinkedIn where it is acceptable to directly message someone on the first message. Remember the rule of contact that was shared earlier and decide what will work for you. In the following scripts, we will share how to use direct messages, posts, stories, and lives to start connections with people.

Let's dive into direct messages you can send to someone in their DIRECT MESSAGE. This seems like a no-brainer, but you may be new to this whole social platform thing. Remember that, on LinkedIn,

SOCIAL MEDIA SCRIPTS

there are people's pages. If you post on their page, it is public, and everyone can see this post. Then there are direct personal messages. Like on other social media platforms, only the person you sent the message to can see it. The following scripts are to be used in direct messages.

The first message in this script should be one of connection. Building QUICK rapport shouldn't take very long. You can quickly go to their profile and find something to make mention of. Just remember to keep it authentic.

Cold messaging is less effective because there is no previous connection or trust. A cold market is a group of people you have no previous connection with. This is the majority of the population. You must quickly build confidence in a cold prospect and catch their attention in a world full of noise and spam.

Many network marketers do not want to handle the rejection of those they know, so they move way too quickly to just their cold market. The reason why so many STRUGGLE recruiting their warm market are for one of these reasons:

- Their warm market has known them their whole life and knows they have never really been successful at anything, business-wise; therefore, they don't take them seriously.

- Warm-market typically wants to see you MAKE MONEY first before they even consider taking a look. This is why we LOVE the cold market so much. Earlier in the book, we talked about how crucial third-party validation is. Third-party validation becomes crucial with your cold market. Refer to the third party invite scripts to know precisely how to invite people to a third-party conversation. Lastly, use the 'warm market' script shared later in this book to quickly experience some QUICK wins and get into the cold market.

The highest income-producing activity is talking to brand new people about your products or business. Adding a cold market can help you increase consistency with talking to new prospects but just make sure it doesn't replace your warm market.

Coach Fryer has worked with many successful leaders, and most would agree that they made a LOT more money after working through their warm market and tapping into the cold market. This helped them make a BRAND NEW first impression with those in the cold market. Your warm market typically doesn't convert as well because they know you too well. They want to wait and see what type of success you have first. Those in the cold market have NO IDEA of your past successes or failures and are typically more open to listening! Below are the scripts we used when approaching people in the cold market.

Here is another framework that you can follow online that will work with every single person. It doesn't matter if it is LinkedIn or any other social media platform. A written message should do three things.

1 - Be genuine and not fake.

2 - Find a point of reference for the friend connection.

3 - Finish with a simple parting phrase or question.

Oh, and a bonus tip that is common sense, DO NOT BE WEIRD.

The scripts for bold first interactions on social media

"Hey, Sally, I am on Linkedin to network and hope you appreciate the fact I am very direct and straight to the point. I have built an online business using social media and am looking to expand my business with other entrepreneurs. I would love for you to take a quick look at the 5 min overview of my business. If it is a fit for you, it may be for someone you know. Would you be open to checking it out?"

"Hey, Sally, I see that you are from Florida and in finance. I was just in Florida 3 months ago for my daughter's tennis tournament. I loved it, but it was the middle of the summer, so I died of humidity. I am in Utah, where there is no humidity. Glad to connect. How long have you been in finance?"

"Hey _____(insert their name)! I thought it would be cool to reach out and connect as we are both in the XYZ group together. I loved the post you made yesterday; it spoke to me! How long have you been in that group?"

"Hi_____I noticed you commented/posted in (XYZ GROUP) and I loved (*insert compliment then end with a question to keep the conversation going*)."

"Hey____fun to connect with you here on LinkedIn. How is your networking going?"

"Hey _____(insert their name)! I realize we've been connected on (insert platform) now for almost a year, and I never connected to say hello! I didn't realize you lived in Texas. We lived there for 5-years ourselves, loved it there! How long have you been there?"

"Hey _____, I know this might sound kinda crazy, but based on the post I saw you make yesterday about struggling with _____(insert problem/pain/issue), I may know of something that can help that's been working for me. Let me know if you'd like more info; if not, no worries."

Here are several easy questions to ask in the first message.

- How is your day going so far?
- How was your weekend?
- How long have you been a fitness trainer?
- How long have you been a member of the XYZ group?

"I hate when people spam others on social media so I wanted to ask you first if you are open to taking a look at _____."

"I know we just connected, but I have had a ton of success with my online business. Most people plug into our simple social media system and work a few hours a week. It may not be for you, but it may be for someone you know. If I send some quick info to check it out, would you check it out and give me your honest feedback?"

"Hey____I would love for you to look at this great opportunity I am a part of. I have created a great second income for my family, and it has been pretty simple. Don't worry if you aren't interested. I won't be one of those annoying people who bug you every day, but I think you are going to be interested."

The lessons from bold first interactions on social media

This is for the people that like to get precisely to the point. They are sending these messages out in high volume. Adapt and mold it to you. Take out the words and phrases that you wouldn't use. Extract the principle, which is to be direct, sell them on taking a look and finishing with the power of connections. This script aims to get people interested in you for the pitch, with little to no personal connection in the beginning. The connection is made through the joint interest in the offer—one note with the super direct approach. You still need to build connections! This doesn't skip the step of building relationships. One person told me they used the super direct approach because they didn't have to get to know anyone. SERIOUSLY?! He missed the point entirely. The super direct approach gives you something to connect around. You always should be and will be creating and building relationships.

You notice how we said, "I hate when people spam." The principle here is to hit your insecurities head-on during your invite. If you are worried about someone thinking this is a network marketing company, hit it head-on. If you are worried about people thinking you will hard close and sell them, hit it head-on. If you are worried that friends will think you will be pushy for the next six months, hit it head-on. This is being authentic. This is where we bring in the obstacle from the very start to overcome it. This is where you need to step up and be the BOLD version of yourself!

If they say yes, you plug them into the tool you use, which could be a quick video or even a FB group. I can't stress this enough. FORTUNE IS IN THE FOLLOW-UP! These scripts only work if you are willing to follow up. If you send the above approach and someone says yes, you may have lost a prospect if you don't follow up. All of these scripts don't stop once you use them. There will ALWAYS be follow-up that needs to happen. Do it promptly and be on the ball with your follow-ups.

Often people read the first message, and they may be interested, but not enough to do anything about it. Following up shows your commitment level and gives them another opportunity to know you. Refer back to the follow-up scripts to see precisely what to say.

Direct messages on Facebook and other social platforms

We don't need to sing the praises of Facebook and Instagram too much. Billions of people post, watch and interact on these two platforms daily. These two platforms are run by the same company and share similar features. But, they also have many differences that can sometimes determine which platform you primarily use. Once again, remember that it doesn't matter what social platform you use; it just matters that you use it.

Cold messaging and direct messaging on social platforms is a numbers game. You will have a lower percentage of people saying yes to your products or business with this method, but this works better for many because they can make more invites consistently. You will be messaging MORE people for the numbers to work in your favor. This would be a great place to do some split testing, as we mentioned at the beginning of the book.

Lastly, remember that the BETTER you become in conversations and master the skill of talking to people and asking the right questions, the HIGHER your conversions will be. At first, you may have to message 25-50 people to get a few responses, but as your confidence grows and your language becomes even better, you may need only to message 10-15 people to get several to say they are OPEN; to learn more! This is where your willingness to try and fail and use the split testing will come into play.

The scripts for direct messages on social media

"Hey Brian, I just sent you a friend request. I saw you are in the same hiking group that I am in. I love hiking. My favorite hike was Trolltunga in Norway this past year. Where's your favorite place you've hiked?"

SOCIAL MEDIA SCRIPTS

"Hey Brian, your name popped up as a suggested friend. How do you know Sally Smith and Mary Joe? It looks like we have a ton of mutual friends in common. I am looking forward to connecting."

"Hey Brian I somehow saw one of your posts about _____. I loved it. I see you are from Florida. I was just there last year. I loved it, but it was mid-summer, so it was crazy humid. I just sent you a friend request. I am looking forward to connecting."

PLEASE NOTE the paragraph below is meant to be a conversation not just a series of questions you ask.

"I saw you were having trouble sleeping. :(I hate knowing you're dealing with that. I had the same issue (or I know someone that did leverage your team members/customer's testimonials/story), and it has been an enormous blessing for me/them. (NOTE: if you have a personal testimony to their issue, it will be more powerful).

- What have you tried to help with that?
- On average, how much would you say you are spending a month to help with that?"

"I have a group with some more info and testimonials. Would you like to check it out?"

"I have this great Facebook group that I know you would love. I am sending you the link. Make sure to fill out the questions, and I will see you inside the group."

"Thanks for joining the group. I went ahead and tagged you in a couple of posts that I think are relevant to what you and I discussed earlier. I didn't want to blow up your notifications completely, but check them out and let me know if you have any questions."

"Just got you added to the group. Would you like the link to the website as well? Sometimes it helps to have some extra resources."

"Do you know anyone who would be open to _____?"

"Do you know anyone who would benefit from_____?"

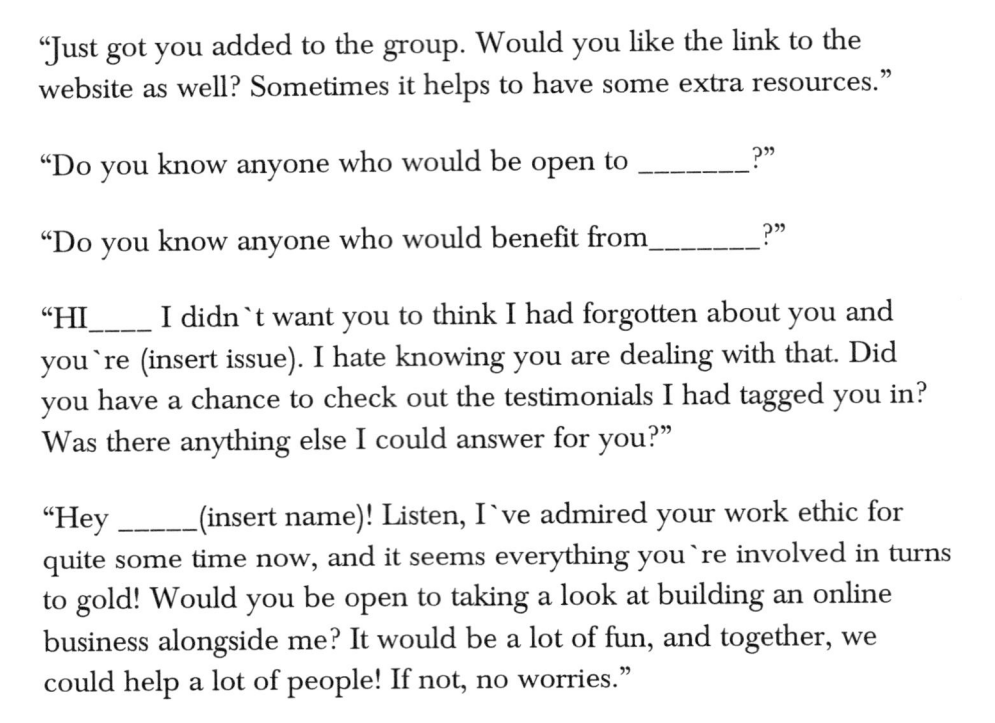

"HI____ I didn`t want you to think I had forgotten about you and you`re (insert issue). I hate knowing you are dealing with that. Did you have a chance to check out the testimonials I had tagged you in? Was there anything else I could answer for you?"

"Hey _____(insert name)! Listen, I`ve admired your work ethic for quite some time now, and it seems everything you`re involved in turns to gold! Would you be open to taking a look at building an online business alongside me? It would be a lot of fun, and together, we could help a lot of people! If not, no worries."

Lessons from direct messages on social media platforms

Regardless of which platform you are on, I recommend sending a message right after sending a friend request to someone. When they see a friend request, this creates interest, and a message pops right up from you when they accept it.

On most social platforms, you can use audio messages. Audio messages are more genuine than they get to hear your voice, but you can send a written message if you insist on not doing voice messages. To increase the likelihood of them listening to it, keep it UNDER 30-seconds. We all know we do the eye roll when we get those long voice texts. Keep it short and sweet to kick this conversation off on the right foot!

It`s worth repeating this when making connections online. First, be genuine and not fake.

Second, find a point of reference for the friend connection. Finally, finish with a simple parting phrase or question. And the bonus tip, DO NOT BE WEIRD.

You may not like any of these variations, but you get the principles to make them your own. Remember to take massive deliberate action. By doing so, you will learn which words and phrases work best for your style. Once again, this works because of consistency. This means the consistency of you showing up and friend requesting people and your consistency of not being weird! If someone gets a voice message from you that is normal and then sees your average hiking group posts, they will start to Know, Like, and Trust you even more. Don't blow it by being weird in your posts, stories, or DM's.

Social Platform Live Launch Videos

We both have A LOT to say about live videos because it has helped us tremendously in our businesses. We have created a quick guide to becoming a pro at video, and then we get right into the scripts that you can use. Remember that people love reality TV shows. A great way to get attention and keep people interested is to do lives where people follow your JOURNEY. It is catchy, and it follows the same format as reality TV. Below we have included several different videos scripts that you can use. The best part is that you can use them in the sequence we have put them in to help create the journey of your business or product that you are sharing.

- Facebook Live interviews give you borrowed credibility and a shared audience.

- Why is it so important? The percentages are constantly changing, but you need to understand that currently, Facebook Lives show much much much more than regular posts or even uploaded videos. There is no better way to build your brand than Facebook Live.

- Practice a few on the ONLY ME Setting. Then delete and practice again. Then go Live.

- You can also practice them in one of your groups. This is usually a more familiar setting.

- Privacy setting must be public.

- When to go Live? Go to FB Messenger to track how many are online every hour for a day. This will give you a gauge.

- Great catchy headline!

- Feel free to edit your headline after your post.

- Mute your phone notifications. I even put my phone in flight mode and then turn on the WiFi when I can.

- I like to start with HIGH ENERGY and create curiosity about what my audience will learn from the rest of Facebook Live. The first 15 seconds are KEY. You are selling them quickly on why they can`t miss this Facebook Live.

- Don`t worry about how many people are on.

- Be authentic. Smile.

- Ask engaging questions.

- Drop a 1 or 2? Give them the option. Which one are you?

- Drop an emoji if...

- STRIVE FOR QUESTIONS THROUGHOUT THAT GET PEOPLE TO COMMENT DURING

- Engage the audience with comments. The interaction will boost how many see it.

SOCIAL MEDIA SCRIPTS

- Find your go-to three friends who will watch Live and comment a ton!

- Start right away! Do the Facebook Live for the replay viewer.

- ALWAYS GIVE STEPS.

- Get to the point. Many people ramble when they are nervous on Facebook Lives.

- Use notes.

- Be hands-free whenever possible so that the video isn't shaking everywhere.

- You will be BAD when you start! That's ok!

- Voice and body language are critical.

- Hold the phone horizontal.

- Look into the camera hole!

- Good lighting (buy a selfie ring or buy some sort of lighting)

- Good WiFi or service (if possible)

- Be consistent. People will watch old ones boosting those posts as you do ones that people like.

- Switch up locations. This isn't a must, but every so often gives them a different look.

- Towards the end of the FB live, I ask for my audience to comment on what they would add or what their most significant insight/reminder is.

- Drop your latest training link in your last 3 Facebook Lives. Erase the last one you made.

- Share RELEVANT content to other GROUPS. Not every video. Don't just Share. Apply the post to the group. Create a call to action to create interest.

- Only share to groups you are engaging in! No one likes the taker!

- Advanced techniques. Go through 15 Facebook Lives. Figure out which ones were your top 4. Go through those top 4 Facebook Lives and see on the wavelength (just click on your live video, and it'll show) to see the dull spots and the most intriguing (high) parts. Find commonalities to learn what engages your audience.

- Your goals are interaction. Comments send shares. And ideally, for others to subscribe to your FB Lives by turning on notifications.

LIVE VIDEO FORMAT:

Title: short, sweet, 8-words or less, goal is to get the IDEAL viewer to click play, hit on ONE pain.

Intro: insert your impact/mission statement (I help _____)

Question/Hook: reiterate the title! Example: Would learning how I lost 10-pounds in the last 30-days be helpful? If so, stick around as I share exactly how I did it."

Content: 2-3 bullet points of helpful/valuable content

CTA: if you don't instruct viewers what to do next, they will do nothing!

SOCIAL MEDIA SCRIPTS

The scripts for live video on social platforms

(VIDEO) "I am so excited and a little bit skeptical. I just ordered these fantastic weight loss products that are supposed to help you sleep better, speed up your metabolism, and curb your appetite. I have tried so many different products and systems that I hope this is the one that finally works. Yes, I know that exercise and eating well are critical, but I still want the extra boost to give me some hope. I am going to keep all of you posted on this system."

(VIDEO) Open your products. Unbox. Don't show your product name.

"Here we go! I am going to open this up. The reason I wanted to try this was that (mention issue or benefit that you were excited about). I had a good friend tell me about it, and I wanted to try it. OH! I love how it comes in this easy-to-take packet. This will make it easy for me to know exactly how many to take. If this does what it says it does, I will be hooked for life. I have been looking for something like this for a long time."

(VIDEO) "Wow, I know that several of you have followed along with me as I started looking into this (product or business). Before sharing my results, I wanted to tell you about (insert name)'s story and why they started. (SHARE SHORT STORY). That leads me to how I got started and where I am today. (Share your story) I will keep sharing with you because I know this is a journey and that I will continue to have fantastic results. If you are interested in learning more, hit me up in my DM's. If I shared everything that this has done, it would be WAY too long, but I am passionate about helping struggling people like me, so don't hesitate to ask questions, and if you are open, I would love to share with you more about this."

(VIDEO) "Hey everyone, _____here. I help_____. Would learning how I lost ten pounds in the last thirty days be helpful? If so, stick around as I share exactly how I did it." After this, share two to three

87

points and offer valuable content. Then tell people EXACTLY what to do next. Make one offer, or they will do nothing!

Lessons from live video on social platforms

Social platform live videos are their very own challenge for most people. Combine not knowing what to say and being on video, and we have created the perfect storm for fear and anxiety. Lives on Facebook, Instagram, or any other platform can be scary. There is no better way to gain exposure and market for free.

In the video, you want to make sure that you talk about the product's benefits. Don't show the company name. Create interest. TEASE them! Always focus on your flagship product or system. Sell the benefit. Be authentic to you and how you are feeling. As always, show PASSION and energy. Passion and energy don't mean you need to turn into some crazy person, but be the most energetic version of yourself. Remember this, energy and enthusiasm are contagious. Don't overcomplicate it. Be ignorance on fire, not knowledge on ice. You don't have to know everything to start, but you do have to take action, and you will learn as you go. Remember that you can do videos on the product and the business once every week. Don't go all spammy doing lives every day about the same thing. The goal is to keep people interested. The best part is that as you start to share your own story with the product or the business, people will want to follow along, so keep giving them well-spaced updates on how it is going.

Instagram/FB Stories

Walt Disney said, "The best way to start is to start doing.`` How to tell a STORY takes AWARENESS and practice. You will need to start doing this before figuring out what gets your audience engaged. Stories only last for 24 hours, so if you have an awful story, who cares?! It will be gone before you know it, and no one will remember it. But, you will have more experience and practice showing up on social media and trying out different ways to engage with your audience.

Figure out five topics that are personal to you. Grab a piece of paper and start by listing everything that interests you. What would you love to spend time talking to people about? This could be a hobby like mountain biking or your obsession with Disney. Write it all down. Next, narrow it down to what you want to talk about the most. Sure, you have baseball cards from when you were a kid, but are you obsessed with them? Do you want to start conversations about it? Find things that you want to post and discuss. One of the five topics should have to do with your business.

You can start by mapping out your week and planning what to post once a day, at least five days a week. This usually means just one post a day on the social media platforms that you are committed to staying consistent. There may be occasional days where you post multiple times, but be careful. People may get annoyed and stop following you because you post too often unless you are an influencer. This goes for POSTS only! People are entirely ok with multiple stories a day if you do stories or reels. They are not only ok with it, but they expect it. So the 5-2 formula compresses a week`s worth of posting with your five main topics and creating at least five stories in one day.

We both love to use the 5-2 FORMULA for stories. Suppose your themes were family, travel, humor, health, and spirituality. Inside those themes, you can and should get more specific. For now, we won`t go into that. To keep it simple, you want to try and compress one whole week of posting into one day, where you create posts to cover your top five topics. You could also focus the five posts on one topic that you will post throughout the week.

THE ULTIMATE SCRIPT BOOK

Here's an example. Let's use a supplement company as an example and focus on one theme.

- Your first story could show you going to the gym.

- Do you prefer lifting weights or cardio? Your second story could show you posting photos at the gym that ask questions via the poll option. By asking a question, you bring your audience into your lives.

- Your third story could show you making your workout shake.

- Your fourth story could show you drinking a ton of water and mentioning how that has been the #1 thing to help you curb your appetite.

- Your fifth story could be asking your audience what time they typically go to bed? This could be a question or a poll.

- Your 6th post could be giving some of your top tips for anything with health.

- Your 7th post could be you going to bed and mentioning your typical time.

This is just one example. As you become consciously aware of these strategies, you will create a location to create notes and store all of your ideas.

How often should you create a STORY? The EVERY HOUR RULE is for the overachievers. No, no, no! I don't mean to post when you are asleep. I am not that crazy. If you posted about every hour throughout the day and ended up with 16 stories, you are at the highest level of stories. Understand this.

Each INDIVIDUAL story lasts 24 hours and then is GONE. Stories currently show based on the most recent story. So if you post every hour, you will constantly be bumped to the front of the line and get much more engagement. They will see your newest story, but they will also see your older stories. Very few are willing to keep up with this strategy, so here is my suggestion. Create a minimum goal and stick with it. Let's say you create the goal with three stories a day. Go into your calendar and set reminders three times a day to help you remember to create that story. Do not check off that reminder until you create your story.

Social Story HACK from Coach Fryer: if you feel your stories' views are stagnant or decreasing, let them EXPIRE! Meaning, don't post any NEW stories for 24hrs. Then on your first story post the next day, add a pic of you, ask a question using text, and include a POLL option to spark engagement! Watch your views double (maybe even triple)! Do this twice per month to reset your views!

Stories are an incredible tool to NURTURE your existing audience further. Stories are NOT meant to grow your friends and followers, but rather connect on a DEEPER level with existing ones. No matter which product or company you are promoting, TRUST is how you earn more business. The more your audience trusts you, the more likely they are to be open to learning more about what you sell or promote. It's okay to be a bit more vulnerable in stories. Providing a good mixture of posts in your stories is also HIGHLY recommended.

Examples:

Post 1 - video clip (enable captions) this should be done a minimum of one per day.

Post 2 - Pic with text and poll

Post 3 - Testimonial, GIF

The scripts for social platform stories

"A day in the life of me! Follow along today and see what I usually do on Tuesdays."

"I was wondering if you all could help me out today. Post in the comments your favorite pick me up in the afternoon."

"So pumped to get another message from a happy customer! That makes my day."

VIDEO: "I wanted to jump on today and just share a message of motivation. I know that in the past, I have found other people's videos like this so helpful. Today I just wanted to remind you that you are worth the effort. You are worth your dreams. You are here to be your unique self, and that is perfect. Hope you all have a great day!"

"Settle this argument at our house for me. Who takes the trash out at your house?"

"Wanted to share a couple of ways I use my products during the day with you. Check out my next couple of stories to see!"

VIDEO: "Today, I am sharing the top five ways to use this product. I always love to see how people use them myself, so I thought I would share how I do....."

The Scripts for follow-up from social platform stories

"Thanks so much for doing my poll about (needing more energy). May I send you some more info on what I found to help with (more energy)? I hope you are well :)."

"I have seen your name pop up in my (notifications/stories etc.), so I thought I would say HI! (find some common ground to connect with them on) ex. Your kids are so cute! How old are they? Mine are 8 and 10 :)."

"Thanks for checking out my stories. Have you seen anything that you would like more information on?"

"Thanks for following me and watching my stuff. It`s great to know that there are actual people out there. LOL. Do you know anyone that could benefit from anything that I have posted? If not, no worries, How is your day going so far?"

"I love that we have connected here. I just thought I would pop over and tell you to thank you for your last post about _____It connected with me."

"Thanks for replying to my question. I shared an answer to my stories. You can check it out right now if you haven`t gotten a chance. If you have any other questions, feel free to DM me. Cheers!"

Lessons on stories

People love reality shows. In my lifetime reality shows became a thing. Now it has become a staple in the entertainment industry. My kids still don`t believe me that reality tv wasn`t a thing when I was a kid. Social media has made reality watching even more personal by letting people get a behind-the-scenes look into everyday people`s lives. Social media "stories" are the behind-the-scenes reality version of your life. It is so fascinating as it is the authentic version of one`s life. It is the fastest way people are now consuming social media and something that you will want to take advantage of. Let`s dive into strategies for social media.

Interaction on STORIES leads to MESSENGER, which boosts your VISIBILITY to that person. This means that FB or Instagram will show your content to those you interact with more.

If you ever feel like you have run out of NEW people to talk to, check to see WHO is watching your stories! This is an excellent opportunity for you to personally connect and MESSAGE those who are not only interacting with your stories but watching them as well!

Done RIGHT stories will be ONE of the most effective tools on SOCIAL MEDIA to generate WARM LEADS. This is YOUR opportunity to nurture all of your existing friends/followers and allow them to get to know you better and ultimately build more trust! We always say "Niches to Riches." This means you don't want to try to be everything to everyone, or you will be nothing to no one. You want to be deliberate and have a focus. We both have more training in our Facebook groups and coaching that you can reference if you have a hard time identifying who you are talking to. For now, just remember that you have to talk to people specifically. It doesn't work to talk to "all the people, all the time." Be focused and deliberate about who you are talking to.

IMPORTANT NOTE - Don't plan on crushing your business just from stories, even great posts or lives. Stories, posts, and lives are just ONE part of social media success. Social media is just ONE part of having a successful business. Don't get fooled into thinking that you can crush your business by posting using one thing every day and become an overnight sensation. By utilizing stories, lives, and posts, you increase your likeability, credibility, recall ability/visibility, leading to profitability. You still need to have conversations with your potential prospects. That's why the MONEY is in MESSENGER!

POSTS ON SOCIAL

There are several different ways to connect on social media. We have just mentioned the benefits and value of using stories and reels, but please don't miss out on posting. Posts should educate, entertain or inspire. Social platforms LOVE when people use all of the available ways of staying social with their audience. Don't focus solely on stories because the algorithm also wants you to make posts. The other reason you want to post is that people will go to get to know you better. Maybe your reel or story came up, and they want to get to know you better. If they go and see that you haven't posted in a year, they may not go any further.

Humor is one of the easiest ways to connect with others. If this doesn't fit your style or personality, don't force humor. But, I will say that your humor can be different and still impact. I recently worked with a woman who had always thought she had a dry sense of humor that people didn't get. She started posting videos and memes on social media using her dry sense of humor, and her engagement exploded!

Remember, your goal is for your personality to stand out to attract those who truly connect with you.

Another thing that you will want to be mindful of is what pictures are getting the most attention and interaction. Here are the pictures we know do amazing with our followers:

- Pictures with our wives or family
- Vacation pictures
- Pictures with other people in network marketing
- Meme relevant to right now
- Fill in the blank

Here are some images that we know do *terrible* on social media across the board.

- Stock photos
- Random pictures of your day with no context on the picture
- Quotes that don't relate to the niche
- Hobby photos that don't interest our niche

Take this list with a grain of salt. We want you to know that after you have been doing this for a while, you will start to notice patterns of pictures and images that your followers like and engage with. Don't ignore this! Start using that information to your advantage and get your followers more engaged by posting engaging images.

The scripts that we have included for posting on social media are different from the scripts that we have shared previously. But we will say that they work! Both of us have very engaging and interactive posts across all social platforms. This didn't happen by accident! We came up with scripts and formulas that work, and we stick to them. We have included some of the scripts we use on social media that have had the biggest engagement on both our accounts and our clients. These scripts can be used with any image that works for your audience. As we mentioned at the beginning of this book, you will want to do split testing to see what works best.

The Scripts

Funny posts- People love to engage in things they find funny. This is one of the fastest ways to connect with people and have them remember you.

"Me: Hey babe, let's go to Victoria's Secret for date night...

Her: We are going to Costco."

"If people are talking behind your back...then just fart."

"Choosing a network marketing compensation plan but a bad product or service is like marrying someone with a great body and no personality!"

"Do not argue with an idiot. He will drag you down to his level and beat you with experience."

"I don't know who needs to hear this, but yes, I am big Pimpin and spendin' G's. Thank you for asking."

Relatable Posts

Be vulnerable but don't be the overly dramatic person that is always making everything a huge deal. People like to know you are also a NORMAL person dealing with the regular everyday challenges that we all deal with.

"This is what happens when Dad is in charge. My four-year-old owns me."

"Please, stop it...Stop thinking you have to have it all figured out. My wife and I used to spend the wee hours of the night plotting how we were gonna live a life of freedom, eventually. We dreamed, we prepared, but most importantly we took imperfect action. Stop living a life of what-ifs, and just do it already."

"I have heard of mom guilt before, but do dads ever feel dad guilt? What does that mean to you?"

"Just spent the past hour going over and over in my head if I was saying "moist," right. "MOY-SSSST." Is that right?"

"I can't believe I still watch AFV as an adult. What is a childhood tv show that you still enjoy watching?"

"How is it that my mom can STILL say my name a certain way, and I know I am in trouble?"

Fun

If you do anything fun at all, post about it. Share the fun. Remember, most people are on social media because they are bored, so entertain them. This goes for anything I once posted about an exciting trip to the grocery store and got tons of engagement. People are curious about how other people live, and they want to see your life. This is especially true post-pandemic. After our world shut down, people are now finding more and more joy every day, so if you are doing something fun, post about it! Let people see what you like doing and who you are doing it with.

"Just got back from _____. I wish you could have been here with us."

"Just had the best experience at____."

"Anybody else spend WAY too much time at the _____?"

"We have always wanted to go to_____. So grateful I was able to have that experience with_____."

"If you were to tell me five years ago that I would be able to do_____I wouldn't have believed you! So awesome to be able to have this experience."

"Finally able to meet up with this legend!"

"A day in the life of us :)."

Positive Posts

No likes the negative nelly—the person who is always negative about everything. You usually just block those people. Share something positive that you believe in.

"The greatest compliment I can receive in network marketing is when someone introduces me as a family man, great friend, or an honest person that has helped them out. This is true success."

"You are closer than you think to change your life. Keep going."

"God, family, business. We are just getting started. Let's do this."

"Those who don't jump will never fly! - Leena Almashat"

"Don't let social media fool you. Nobody's life is perfect. We are all doing the best we can, and our best is good enough."

"Never be a prisoner of your past. It was just a lesson, not a life sentence."

Fill in the blank

This is a great way to spark engagement that goes beyond the "like" or "heart." People love to fill in the blank (we blame Mad Libs ;). So if you are looking to get more people to comment, try one of these posts. It is a simple way to engage with your audience.

"Money is_____."

"My next vacation is_____."

"Something that few people know about me is_____."

"If I had one wish I would_____."

"My biggest dream is to_____."

"If I could have lunch with anyone, it would be_____."

Capitalize on trends

There are always quick trends that pop up on social media. Jump on those trends and then, if you can, try to stand out to be a little bit different from the crowd. Make sure you create these quickly.

"Well, I decided to jump on the bandwagon and show you my profile pic from nine years ago and then a photo from a few months ago."

"How it started vs. How it`s going."

"I can`t believe my kids got me to do this. Here goes nothing."

"How old is too old to get on the _____ bandwagon?"

"I just had to try this out! What do you think?"

Expert tips

Many of you struggle with this because you don`t feel qualified to be the expert yet. That`s ok. Use borrowed credibility. Borrow a fact, stat, or quote, and then share your insight on it. The objective is to be seen as helpful and can be turned to for advice or expert insight.

"Surround yourself with such a strong environment that it is impossible to fail."

"After years of experience, I can safely say that I am quite the expert at_____. Here are my top three tips on _____. ADD TIPS."

"I haven`t always known how to_____. But I want to share with anyone else who might be struggling with what I have found to help. I wish I would have found a post like this when I was going through it."
ADD TIPS

"Top three ways to CRUSH the competition at_____."
SHARE tips

"One study shows that 87% of people don't love their jobs.

You may not be striving to be a millionaire, but understand that 80% of millionaires own their own business, and although they work hard, they don't work that many more hours than MANY full-time employees.

I only give you these statistics to show that dreams take WORK, VISION, and TIME."

Caption this post

It could be a photo of YOU, or it could be of someone else. Anything that you think could get a wide range of funny responses. This gets people to stay and think about your post more. It also helps because people want to stay on your post and read the other responses. The key to this post is to find a great engaging picture, and then the script is easy.

"Caption this post...."

The list post

People love lists! They are very engaging. It is an excellent way for others to get to know you and also for them to share their opinions.

"The five best TV theme songs of all time...."

"Top 10 most life-changing books I have ever read...."

"The top three places I have ever been in the world...."

"Top eight things to NEVER say to your wife when she is hungry...."

"The SEVEN biggest fails I ever had...."

Engaging questions

"What's the best book you have read in the last year?"

"What is your favorite movie of all time?"

"What is the most overrated food?"

"What is the best gift you have ever gotten?"

"What is the first thing you do in the morning when you wake up?"

Product Testimonials

This is a great way to create curiosity with your products. We are not fans of blasting your product's name all over social media. If people are interested, they will do their research or reach out to ask you. The best commercials tell stories and evoke emotion. We know facts tell, and stories sell, so learn to share real authentic stories. Make them more value-based. There is no need to pitch others or tell them to message you unless you send samples. They know they can message you. That screams salesy and spammy.

"You would DIE if I told you what I have struggled with for so long. Since I have found an excellent solution, I am not as shy about talking about it." Share testimonial of the product such as:

"I never thought I would be THAT GUY talking so openly about something I use, but here I am. I guess I am a social influencer now. LOL." Share two sentences about the product for example:

"You all know that I take recommendations very seriously. I am pretty sure I missed my calling as an expert YELP reviewer. That being said, I have to share this product with you."

"I can't imagine my life without this amazing_____. I use it every single day. Have you ever tried it before?"

Examples of good business curiosity posts

When creating a business post, you must remember that the principle is similar to product testimonials. You want to create curiosity, be less salesy/spammy, and tell good stories. That's it! It is that easy. So often, people get stuck because of stories they are telling themselves about what people will think if they talk about a product or opportunity.

"It was fun spending time with awesome entrepreneurs. I can't wait to do our next meet-up and talk about our businesses."

"It makes a difference as a business owner having other entrepreneurs to work and collaborate with. So grateful for a company that creates so many opportunities to learn and succeed with others."

"I still can't believe I own my own business. It has been a crazy epic ride. The best part is that I am just getting started. Let's GO!"

"It's possible. It is possible to grow a business to whatever you want. It's possible to have time freedom. It's possible to create epic vacations for the family. I am grateful that I believed in the possibility and got after it."

"Shoutout to (team member name). He has done an incredible job creating HUGE success in his business this month. Nobody can stop this freight train!"

Lessons from posts on social platforms

#1 The best strategy by far is to create notes on your phone to store every idea about what to post on social media. Any time you think of something funny, insightful, motivational, or anything that would make for a good post, put it in your notes right away. This one strategy made all of the difference for me because some days, I just can't think of anything to post. This goes for tracking who is engaging with your posts as well. If you notice that you have someone who likes and comments on your posts, write their name down. That may be someone you want to do some research on and reach out and connect with.

We know that posting on social media can feel overwhelming. Sometimes it can feel like you are talking to yourself or that your voice is getting drowned out amongst the masses on social media. If we could encourage you to do one thing, it would be just to keep going. Consistency determines success. If you stay committed to consistency, you will see success follow. Posting on social media is also a great way to improve your messaging and voice. Don't get stuck looking at your "likes" or "comments"; focus on your consistency.

CONCLUSION

Network marketing doesn't have to be complicated. We will end this book as we started it; by reminding you that the very best people just learn how to do the basics better. Scripts keep it basic. There is a script for everything you need right here in this book. Use them. Start to see what sounds and feels good to you. Tweak and make these your own. Infuse your personality into them. This book was so much fun for both of us to work on. We found and created the best scripts that will help you throughout the process with prospects in network marketing.

The number one thing that has people quit this business is fear. Please don't be that person! Don't stay stuck in fear of talking to other people. Using these scripts will help you build your confidence in network marketing and help you take the guesswork out of what to say in any situation with your business.

People like to connect with real genuine people. Scripts are great, but they are excellent when you infuse yourself into them. Whether it's online or in-person, people are craving connection. As you work on what to say, make sure that you are also working on it. Look people in the eyes in person. Don't become distracted by other things around you. Pay attention to who you are speaking to. If you are online, make sure to connect and get to know the person. Let them know you. Follow up promptly, and always be kind.

We are both so passionate about helping people win and build successful businesses that bless their lives and the lives of others. We want you to be successful. We want you to know that anyone can succeed in this business if they continue to try and adjust when needed. We have dedicated our entire business to helping people in network marketing win. Network marketing has been a huge blessing for both of us, and we want it to be that way for you too. Use this book to create small successes that will lead to a huge business that will impact your life forever. If you have liked this book and want to connect, please follow us at @robsperry and @coach_fryer on your favorite social platforms.

CPSIA information can be obtained
at www.ICGtesting.com
Printed in the USA
BVHW031915100622
639494BV00013B/454